Sumedha Bhandari

Toni Morrison's Art

A Humanistic Exploration of *The Bluest Eye* and *Beloved*

Anchor Academic
Publishing

Bhandari, Sumedha: Toni Morrison's Art. A Humanistic Exploration of *The Bluest Eye* and *Beloved*, Hamburg, Anchor Academic Publishing 2017

Buch-ISBN: 978-3-96067-118-3
PDF-eBook-ISBN: 978-3-96067-618-8
Druck/Herstellung: Anchor Academic Publishing, Hamburg, 2017

Bibliografische Information der Deutschen Nationalbibliothek:
Die Deutsche Nationalbibliothek verzeichnet diese Publikation in der Deutschen
Nationalbibliografie; detaillierte bibliografische Daten sind im Internet über
http://dnb.d-nb.de abrufbar.

Bibliographical Information of the German National Library:
The German National Library lists this publication in the German National Bibliography.
Detailed bibliographic data can be found at: http://dnb.d-nb.de

© Anchor Academic Publishing, Imprint der Diplomica Verlag GmbH
Hermannstal 119k, 22119 Hamburg
http://www.diplomica-verlag.de, Hamburg 2017
Printed in Germany

For my little munchkins...

Kavya and Aariv

ACKNOWLEDGEMENTS

My explorations in the field of literature would not have been feasible without a generous push of my parents. I take this opportunity to thank my father who, with his keen interest in reading, gently steered me into the world of literature, thus, initiating my never-ending friendship with books. I thank my mother for being my biggest supporter and critic; picking me and helping me gather my selves, whenever times demanded. I thank my brother for being my confidante and my biggest inspiration. I also want to thank my husband for providing me the space to grow and discover myself.

My acknowledgements will remain incomplete without me extending gratitude to my teachers who chiseled me with much care and thought. My mentor, Dr T S Anand, who not only nurtures my interest in literature, but also straightens me when lassitude overpowers my senses; Dr Tejinder Kaur, who inspires me to embrace positivity and reaffirms my faith in humanity; and Dr Nirmal Bajaj, who gently sailed me through this current project.

I have been truly blessed to have come across remarkable teachers who were not only masters of their art but were good human beings as well. I wish to thank all of them for initiating a new thought process in my life.

CONTENTS

THE UNSPOKEN LEXIS OF TONI MORRISON'S NOVELS

Toni Morrison, the eighth American to receive the Nobel Prize in Literature, was born Chloe Anthony Wofford. Her family had migrated North to escape racial prejudice and to seek educational and employment opportunities. In Ohio, Morrison was predominantly surrounded by racist whites. However, this did not impede her growth and success. She attended Lorain High School, where she excelled as a student. She was a member of the student council, worked in the school library (an honor at her school), and was an associate editor of the high school yearbook. She graduated with honors.

Morrison attended Howard University in Washington, D.C., one of the nation's oldest and most prestigious colleges. There she was shocked to find ostentation among the students around her. Most people seemed interested in socializing, their physical appearance, and going to parties. Morrison was mostly concerned with her studies and sometimes found it difficult to find a place at Howard. People had trouble pronouncing her name, so she shortened it to her middle name, Anthony. This later became her now accepted name, "Toni." She majored in English and minored in classics. While at school, she showed interest in the theater and became a member of the Howard University Players, the campus theatrical company. After graduating from Howard, she received a Master's degree in English from Cornell University in 1955. From there, Morrison went to Texas Southern University in Houston, to teach introductory English.

In 1957, Morrison returned to Howard as a member of the faculty where she had the opportunity to teach and to meet many students who later became famous writers and civil rights activists. Some of these students included: the poet Amiri Baraka; Mayor of Atlanta, Andrew Young; civil rights activist and leader of the Student Nonviolent Coordinating Committee (SNCC), Stokely Carmichael; and finally the famous writer, Claude Brown.

At Howard, Morrison met and fell in love with an architect from Jamaica, Harold Morrison. They were married in 1958 and had their first son, Harold Ford, in 1961. Although her marriage was not complete bliss, Morrison and her husband stayed together for six years. In 1964, the family moved to Europe and Morrison became pregnant with her second child. However, by the time she returned from

Europe, her marriage had ended. She attributes her marriage failure to the cultural differences between her and her husband. When Morrison returned from Europe, she moved to Syracuse, New York, where she worked as an associate editor with a textbook subsidiary of Random House. She worked hard during the days and came home to parent her two sons. Then, at night, she would work on her writing, and specifically, the book that would bring her world acclaim, The Bluest Eye. Morrison drew on many of her own life experiences and memories growing up in Lorain, Ohio to write this first book. After twenty years of editing for Random House, Morrison left in 1984 to become a professor at the State University of New York in Albany. She worked there for five years, working on many literary pieces. But in the spring of 1989 she left and became the first African-American woman writer to hold a named chair at an Ivy League university. She was named the Robert F. Goheen Professor in the Council of Humanities at Princeton University. She taught in the creative writing program, and participated in the African-American studies, American studies, and women's studies departments. Her plethora of work includes novels like The Bluest Eye (1970), Sula (1973), Song of Solomon (1977), Tar Baby (1981), Beloved (1987), Jazz (1992), Paradise (1998), Love (2003); miscellaneous writings like: Dreaming Emmet (performed 1986, but unpublished), Playing in the Dark: Whiteness and the Literary Imagination (1992), Remember: The Journey to School Integration (2004); and for children, with son Slade Morrison she wrote: The Big Box (1999), The Book of Mean People (2002), The Lion or the Mouse? (2003), The Ant or the Grasshopper? (2003), and The Poppy or the Snake (2004).

Before customizing the work of Toni Morrison it is necessary to delineate the character of Afro-American fiction. It is primarily a social treatise which deals with the social, psychological and humanistic milieu. It is a microcosm of the entire Afro-American existence. It has a plot, a structure, a language intertwined with cultural symbols, patterns, beliefs and practices and the author's point of view or vision. Through their pen Afro-American writers try to comprehend the overwhelming nature of life. Afro-American women writers in the seventies and eighties like Alice Walker, Paule Marshall, Gloria Naylor, Alexis De Veau have been able to explore the self as central rather than marginal entity. Early Afro- American writers like Zora Neale Hurston, Frances Harper, Jessica Fauset, Nella Larsen and Ann Petry had also tried their hand in this direction. Quest for personal freedom, demand for respect and a desire for a self, were the major themes for these novelists.

Toni Morrison is, perhaps the most formally sophisticated novelist in the history of African-American literature who astutely describes aspects of human lives. There are many writers in the world who are willing to describe the ugliness of the world, Morrison shows her uniqueness and exquisiteness by revealing the hope and beauty that underlines this ugliness. Her artistic excellence lies in achieving a perfect balance between black literature and writing what is universally true. Although firmly grounded in the cultural heritage and social concerns of black Americans, her work transcends narrowly prescribed conceptions of ethnic literature, exhibiting universal mythical patterns and overtones. Her novels, thus, mourn on universal concerns. The signal accomplishment of Toni Morrison as a writer is that she has managed uncannily to invert her own mode of literary representation. Her themes are often those expected of naturalistic fiction-the burdens of history, the determining social effects of race, gender, or class-but they are also the great themes of lyrical modernism-love, death, betrayal, and burden of individual responsibility for her or his own fate. Like Golding, her novels have a fabulistic quality as she has been directly influenced by Afro-American folktales. Like George Eliot she has a rare gift for characterization. She can compel her readers to learn about themselves by experiencing through her characters, their states of mind which they would ordinarily disavow. As a result of her literary and artistic abilities and competence, Toni Morrison stands in the vanguard of contemporary writers of fiction, transcending both her racial identity and gender.

Her first novel, <u>The Bluest Eye</u> (1970), received mixed reviews, didn't sell well, and was out of print by 1974. Critical recognition and praise for Toni Morrison grew with each novel. Her second novel <u>Sula</u> (1973), made both the critics and readers pay attention to her. She received the National Book Critics Circle Award for her third novel <u>Song of Solomon </u>(1977) and the Pulitzer prize for <u>Beloved </u>(1987). She received the Nobel Prize for Literature in 1993 for, in the words of the Swedish Academy, her "visionary force and poetic import" which give "life to an essential aspect of American reality." On October 7, 1993, Toni Morrison became the eighth woman and first black woman to be awarded the Nobel Prize in Literature. When she learned of the honor, she said: "This is a palpable tremor of delight for me."[1]

Toni Morrison believes in the function of the novel as the medium that gives voice to the unheard, unspoken lives of the black people. Morrison wants her prose to recreate black speech, "to restore the language that black people spoke to its original power"[2]; for her, language is the thing that black people love so much--the saying of words, holding them on the tongue, experimenting with them, playing with them. It's a love, a passion. Its function is like a preacher's: to make you stand up out of your seat, make you lose yourself and hear yourself. The worst of all possible things that could happen would be to lose that language. Her prose has the quality of speech; Morrison deliberately strives for this effect, to produce literature that speaks rather than reads. She hears her prose as she writes, and during the revision process she cuts phrasing which sounds literary or written rather than spoken. She rejects critics' assertions that her prose is rich; to those who say her prose is poetic, she responds that metaphors are natural in black speech. Her strong ties to her black culture and oral tradition create a rich foundation for her novels. For Morrison, "all good art has been political"[3] and the black artist has a responsibility to the black community. She aims at capturing the unknown entity that defines what makes a book 'black' oblivious of the fact whether the people in the books are black or not. She thinks that one characteristic of black writers is a constant hunger and disturbance that never ends. Her novels are a reflection of the experiences of the black community and blacks in general. Her work suggests who survived under what circumstances and why, who were the supposed fugitives, what was legal in the community as opposed to what was legal outside it. In The Salon Interview taken by Zia Jaffrey, she asserts: "I'm very much interested in how African-American literature is perceived in this country, and written about, and viewed. It's been a long, hard struggle, and there's a lot of work yet to be done."[4]

Morrison wants readers to be a part in her novels, to be involved actively. Readers are encouraged to craft the novel with her and to help assemble meaning. She uses the model of the black preacher who requires his parishioners to speak, to join him in the sermon, to behave in a certain way, and to accede, change or to modify. She wants readers to say the final prayer. Thus, her writing is meant as a communal experience, a sharing of passion and ideas and responses, with her holding the reader's hand during the experience. One small example of her encouraging reader participation is her not using adverbs so that the reader should recognize and feel the speaker's emotion by feeling the words.

The endeavor in this book is to scrutinize the unspoken lexis of Toni Morrison's works and to unveil the layers of humanistic concerns that provide denotations to her words. Earlier studies on this writer have concentrated on adjudging her as a writer addressing problems of black people. However, this study would try to extend this notion to encompass the problems of whole human community by assimilating blacks in the general drama of life. Before dyeing the strings of Morrison's novels with the colour of humanist concerns, it is important to delineate the term 'Humanism' from which these humanistic concerns arise.

"Humanism stresses the importance of the individual human personality and its power to learn from suffering and to rise above circumstances and in the process it takes cognizance of the paradox that lies at the root of life - the individual is part and parcel of the cultural environment that shapes him, while the self is always in conflict with the culture that shapes him."[5] Its aim is to allow human values to guide one's course in life and affirm those "universal truths" that transcend dogmatism and parochialism. It acts as a counter to all types of authoritarianism, intolerance, loss of self, alienation, atomization, and gradual deterioration from the level of the human to the mechanical or the animal. Humanism, as Kurtz[6] puts it, is life affirming and not life-denying; it seeks to elicit the possibilities of life, and establish the conditions of a satisfactory life for all and not only a few. It grounds humanitarianism, providing foundations for a normative critique as well as explanation of social conditions.

Humanism is a philosophy that affirms the dignity of each individual and supports maximum individual freedom within the framework of social and planetary responsibility. Humanists believe in individual rights and freedoms - but believe that individual responsibility, social cooperation and mutual respect are just as important.

> What a piece of art is a man! How noble in reason! how
> infinite in faculties!
> In form and moving, how express and admirable! In action,
> how like angel!
> In apprehension how like god! the beauty of the world!
> the paragon of animals![7]

Humanism emphasises the dignity of man and his perfectibility. With the essential focus on man and his activities, it considers the world a legitimate object of interest and 'Love' wherein reason tends to soar above revelation. Even Greek writer Socrates shows that God is not necessarily the source of good, or even good himself. Socrates asks if something is good because God ordains it, or if God ordains it because it is already good. It is thus quite natural that the Greeks held in great esteem the heroism of Prometheus who stole fire from the gods in order to preserve mankind. A saviour of man and a rebel against an oppressive god, Prometheus is chained for eternity by Power and Force. Albert Camus in <u>Myth of Sisyphus</u>, shows how Sisyphus returns each time to roll the stone up the hill not in despair but with a smile of scorn hurling defiance to the gods. During Renaissance, when great emphasis was placed on a man-centred universe, it was John Milton who, with bold strokes of his poetic genius, created Satan, the embodiment of evil and yet an incarnation of the defiant spirit of man. Endowed with all the human attributes of both good and evil, he asserts: "the mind is in its own place and in itself can make a Hell of Heaven, a heaven of Hell."[8] Satan here boldly proclaims: "To reign is worth ambition. Better to reign in Hell than to serve in Heaven,"[9] thus making *Paradise Lost* an immortal epic where the spirit of humanism reigns supreme.

With the advent of the industrial revolution and unprecedented technical advancement, new dimension were added to the concept of humanism. Karl Jaspers in his <u>Man in the Modern Age</u> offers a powerful indictment of the progress of the contemporary technological civilization, which he regards as a social disease. Jaspers felt that ever-growing reliance upon objective criteria of thought would have to be paid for by ever- deepening ignorance of the real nature of human existence. It can, thus, be by far emphasized that there is nothing beyond man himself that can solve the problem of man's existence. Soren Kierkegaard offered new perspectives to the humanist thought by focusing attention on Man, in the total, unfathomable inwardness of his being. Kierkegaard bases his position upon individual man here and now, man in his passion and anxiety. Man as a being with a passion for an eternal happiness. He pointed out that genuine critical dilemmas of the individual's life are not solved by intellectual exploration of the facts nor of the laws of thinking about them. Their resolutions emerge through conflicts and tumults in the soul, anxieties, agonies, of faith into unknown territories. The reality of every one's existence proceeds from the inwardness of man, not from anything that the mind can codify. [10]

Jean Paul Sartre recounts in his lecture <u>Existentialism and Humanism</u> that though man's fate is simply to perish, man can triumph over it by inventing "purposes" or "projects," which will themselves confer meaning both upon himself and upon the world of objects-all meaningless otherwise and in themselves. W.H. Auden's exhortation to writers, poets and intellectuals caught in the grip of a life characterized by anxiety and dismay admirably reflects the humanistic concerns of a sensitive soul in combating individual, social and historical crises:

> Sing of human unsuccess
> In a rapture of distress;
> In the deserts of the heart
> Let the healing fountain start,
> In the prison of his days
> Teach the free man how to praise.[11]
>
> *(In Memory of W.B Yeats)*

Derek Walcott is probably right when he says how a writer through "creative schizophrenia" can turn the fragmented cultural legacy occasioned by colonialism into a source of strength rather than divisiveness. In one of his fictional observations, Arun Joshi writes that "life's meaning lies not in the glossy surfaces of our pretensions but in those dark mossy labyrinths of the soul that languish forever."[12]

Keeping these fundamentals in mind this book will proceed towards its aim of analyzing Toni Morrison's work. It is important to note here that no brand or philosophy is being followed here. The concern is with the human part in the word 'humanism'. Humanistic concerns are those concerns that arise out of the consciousness of humanism, the consciousness of man being the central focus and the consciousness of him having the right to lead a respectable life. The concerns of a normal man, woman, and child in the hostile sociological topography are being explored. In this respect, humanism holds a solid ground in the writings of Toni Morrison. Her novels like <u>The Bluest Eye, Sula, Beloved</u> and many more, explore the conditions of men, women and children in the face of hostility and alienation from the outside world. In the Afterword of her novel, <u>The Bluest Eye</u>, Morrison beautifully portrays this point:

> The assertion of racial beauty was not a reaction to the
> self-mocking, humorous critique of cultural/racial
> foibles common in all groups, but against the
> damaging internalization of assumptions of immutable
> inferiority originating in an outside gaze.[13]

The notion of "twoness", a divided awareness of one's identity, was introduced by W.E.B. DuBois, one of the founders of the National Association for the Advancement of Colored People (NAACP).and the author of the influential book The Souls of Black Folks: "One ever feels his two-ness - an American, a Negro; two souls, two thoughts, two unreconciled stirrings: two warring ideals in one dark body, whose dogged strength alone keeps it from being torn asunder."[14]

In her Nobel Lecture Morrison gives voice to the predicament of alienated individuals present in her novels.

> Tell us what it is to be a woman so that we may know what
> it is to be a man. What moves at the margin. What it is
> to have no home in this place. To be set adrift from the
> one you knew. What it is to live at the edge of towns
> that cannot bear your company. [15]
> *(Nobel Lecture, 1993)*

Morrison's style combines these unrealistic elements with a realistic presentation of life and characters. This mixture has been called "magical realism." Initially she objected to the label magical realism, feeling it diminished her work or even dismissed it. Now, however, she acknowledges that it does identify the supernatural and unrealistic elements in her writing. In The Bluest Eye the "magical" appears in the failure of marigolds to bloom and the belief by some members of the community in Soaphead Church's powers. The juxtaposing of the unrealistic with realistic make her novels depict true image of life. This magic realism helps us identify with her characters, their pains, their sorrows, their happiness, their living.

The solution to the dilemma of man to belong is answered by Morrison by her assertion of past and memory as an integral part in man's life. She believes that if a man reclaims his past and his heritage the whole question of belonging will be answered. Morrison says she wrote Beloved convinced that:

> This has got to be the least read of all the books I'd
> written because it is about something that the characters
> don't want to remember, I don't want to remember,
> black people don't want to remember, white people
> don't want to remember. I mean it's national amnesia.[16]

For Morrison black history is the core of black identity. In <u>Beloved,</u> Sethe the protagonist is a victim of sexist and racist oppression. The story is narrated through a series of flashbacks. Morrison is not only concerned with what history had recorded in the slave narratives but what it has omitted, the unvoiced past. This unspeakable past if not claimed will create an unspeakable present and future.

With <u>Sula</u> *(1973)*, the black cultural past is represented by the family, Sula's mother and Grandmother Hannah and Eva Peace, and by Bottom, the community in which they live. In her search for identity and self-definition, <u>Sula</u> *(1973)* chooses to reject her past and to define herself in opposition to her family and community. In the present novel, thus Morrison uses the past-cultural, political and familial- as both revealing and healing for her characters.

In psychological assessment of characters and their lives, Morrison is akin to Camus, Kafka and the likes, yet she is diverse as well. She affords an answer to the problems of her characters. Unlike Camus and Kafka, Morrison does not leave the readers with a pessimist outlook. Her characters are given an answer and though good may not come to the always but there is always a scope for finding answers.

Thus, Morrison's writing endeavors can be perfectly adjudged against the backdrop of humanism. Her fictional characters are constantly engaged in perplexing struggles to maintain their human dignity and emotional sensitivity in an impersonal, alien and frequently threatening world. As the epitaph in her <u>Love</u> [17] *(2003)* claims:

> It takes a lifetime
> to read a face behind a face
> And ages to decipher
> words behind a talk.

In the following chapters this study aspires to bring forth the relationships those different characters in Toni Morrison's novels share with one another. The dissertation is divided into four chapters. The introductory chapter has tried to place Toni Morrison in the literary tradition of women writings, and establish the interconnectedness of race, gender and class which, as systems of societal and psychological restrictions, have critically affected the face of human existence. The chapter has also traced her biography and various literary and cultural experiences that have shaped her fictional art. The second chapter deals with Toni Morrison's first novel, <u>The Bluest Eye</u>, in which the emphasis is on the devastating effects of the beauty standards of the dominant culture on the self-image of a female adolescent. Toni Morrison gets across a very powerful idea that is found in every society today. Although the book is written during the 1940's and most of the events that occur mirror that time period, the main idea transcends to this day and age. With a persuasive argument in mind and a poor, innocent black girl to appeal to the reader's pathos, Morrison craftily writes her story. She uses the rhetorical knowledge that arguments are often improved through the use of sensory details that allow us to see the reality of a problem or through stories that make specific cases and instances come alive. Morrison's argument is how influential society can be on an individual and how strongly its ideas and views are impressed upon that individual. The ideas and views that she speaks of mostly pertain to beauty and what makes an individual beautiful. This idea of beauty can turn someone's life upside down and in the end lead them to madness. Thus, Morrison is trying to impress upon her readers what a negative effect society's ideas and views can have on an individual and how that individual's life is changed forever. Morrison has written of desolation and decay, because this is where, as victims of our environments, we are left. It is a tragedy that Pecola had to undergo such gruesome chain of events. Again redressing the causal argument, society has a standard of beauty; Pecola does not meet this standard. Her life is plagued by event after event which impresses her ugliness upon her. She becomes the object of hatred by all of the members of her town. Her unstable family life leads to her rape which further enhances the problem. Pecola then becomes pregnant and begins her descent towards madness. Her life is then changed forever; she will never be the same. At the end of the book, one of the main characters, Claudia, reflects as an adult that people need someone like Pecola in their lives.

The contention is that what fate lies for Pecola has its genesis in her upbringing and in her parents' insecure attitude in life. The dilemmas and predicaments are transferred in the blood of Pecola. While probing the liaison between her parents; her parents and society, and the society and black people in general, the study has strived to show the general decay and degradation that has marred our society. Pecola suffers because her parents suffered and Pecola's child died because no life could survive in such hostile, alienated environment. Estrangement of a small girl by this insensitive society is enough to unsurface the grisly face of the social order.

The third chapter is concerned with <u>Beloved</u> where Morrison's primary focus is how whites had used every weapon in their armory to devastate the blacks and to keep them fettered in the eternal inferno of slavery. One of the primary themes of <u>Beloved</u> is the issue of race and effects of slavery. Much of the novel focuses on a community of ex-slaves and how they manage to get on track with their lives. The novel questions, through the eyes of schoolteacher, what the difference is between a man and an animal. In its vivid portrayal of the Negro community, complete with their desires and troubles, the novel shows that a colored man is like any other man. The novel also addresses the concern of whether it is better to endure the injustices of an unfeeling people or to fight against them.

Closely tied to the theme of race is that of the past. Each of the characters have endured a furious past, complete with the worst horrors imaginable. Sethe has been raped and forced to murder, Paul D has been imprisoned in a cube in a ditch, Stamp Paid was forced to give his wife away to be a sex toy, and the list goes on and on. Many of these men and women have chosen, like Sethe and Paul D, to repress the past. Others worked actively against it, like Stamp Paid. However, no sort of resolution occurs for any of the characters until each learns to accept and deal with the past (which is very alive in the present). Only then can a future be found. Another humanistic apprehension in <u>Beloved</u> is that of the banality of evil. Slavery is not just an institution; it is a philosophy and mindset which is far-reaching in its consequences. The Garners treated their slaves well, and consequently were respected by such people as Sethe and Paul D. However even then they were mere toys in the hands of their masters. The theme also comes up in the description of the Bodwin's household, which includes the statue of a black boy and the words meaning at your service. The Bodwins have taken an active stance in the fight against slavery, yet fail to comprehend the mindset behind that statue. With such images, Morrison demonstrates the extent of slavery and what must be done to abolish it completely.

The focus is that the moral ambiguity, of course, plays a large role in the novel. The question of, was the murder right or wrong? crops up many times in the book. The answer finally reached is that it was the right thing to do, but Sethe didn't have the right to do it. Had she not murdered Beloved, her and all the children would have been sold back into slavery. Yet, when she committed the murder, she was shunned by an entire community and placed at the mercy of a vengeful spirit. With this comes the larger question of what it means to be free. Was Baby Suggs truly free, when white men were allowed to barge into her yard at any time? Was Paul D free, though he wasn't allowed to love whatever he wanted to love? Were any of the Negroes truly free, who had to wait at the back of the supermarket for the whites to be served before they could get their groceries? Freedom, Morrison points out, is more than a matter of not belonging to a single master.

Another humanistic concern of a well bound of family is also explored in this chapter. Most of the slaves have been torn apart from their families at an early age, and there is little hope in discovering what is left of their families. The consequences of this type of separation can be seen in Sethe, who is possessive of her children, and Paul D, who is determined not to love anything too much. Crisis is also manifested in a loss of values and a breakdown of social and religious institutions. In direct response to Beloved's murder and the slave catcher's threat, Baby Suggs relinquishes her role as the community's spiritual leader. As a result, the community's religious underpinnings falter, threatening it with a deepening of the crisis. Beloved gives testimony to the pain that all the slave women and their descendants have suffered and will suffer. According to Wilfred Samuels and Clenora Hudson-Weems, Morrison has decided that she must "`rip the veil' behind which the slave narrator was forced to hide." Morrison, as Hudson-Weems and Samuels point out, must also reconstruct the narrative of the slave woman, whose story is seldom recorded and then not fully. She provides "the avenue for a resurrected female slave narrator's voice."[18] (Weems, 97-98). The story that Toni Morrison's Beloved tells is, in her narrator's words, "not a story to pass on." Molly Abel Travis writes that Morrison reminds us that we must "embrace the wholeness of our personal histories and cultural histories; we must remember even those parts we would most like to forget."(Weems, 18)

While offering a summing up of the main argument of the dissertation, the last chapter shows how an evolutionary pattern emerges as Toni Morrison, with her heightened consciousness treats, in the course of her novels oppression of black people in white America. The major focus is the oppression of a human being at the hands of grisly society. The theme of humanistic issues is fully addressed in the works of Toni Morrison. Her narrative structures are shaped to imbibe these themes and pose the questions of why and how.

REFERENCES

1. ToniMorrisonNobelLecture.<http://www.nobel.se/literature/laureates/1993/morrison-lecture.html>.
2. ToniMorrisonHomePage.http://www.luminarium.org/contemporary/ tonimorrison.
3. ToniMorrisonHomePage.<http://www.luminarium.org/contemporary/tonimorrison>.
4. Salon.com: Great Books Online. <http://www.archive.salon.com/books/int/1998/02/cov_si_02int>.
5. Mira Panigrahi, Humanism and Culture. New Delhi: Concept, 2001. 20. All subsequent references indicated parenthetically are to this book.
6. Paul Kurtz. <http://en.wikipedia.org/wiki/Secular_Humanism>.
7. William Shakespeare. Hamlet. Ed. M.M. Reese. New Delhi: Kalyani Publishers, 2001, Act ii sc. ii.
8. John Milton. Paradise Lost Books I and II. Ed. F.T. Prince. Delhi: Oxford University Press, 1984. 254-55.
9. John Milton. Paradise Lost Books I and II. Ed. F.T. Prince. Delhi: Oxford University Press, 1984. 263.
10. Nibir K. Ghosh. "Prespectives and Challenges". Humanism in Indian English Fiction. Eds. T.S Anand etc. Creative New Literature Series-78, 2005. 20. All subsequent references indicated parenthetically are to this book.
11. W. H. Auden: Collected Poems. Ed. Edward Mendelson. New York: Vintage Books, 1991. lines 61-65.
12. Sujata Mathai. "An Interview with Arun Joshi". The Times of India. July 7, 1983. 8.
13. Toni Morrison, The Bluest Eye. Vintage, 1999, 168. All subsequent references indicated parenthetically are to this text.
14. W.E.B. DuBois. The Souls of Black Folk. New York: Avon Books, 1965. 14.
15. ToniMorrisonNobelLecture. <http://www.nobel.se/literature/laureates/1993/morrison-lecture.html>.
16. ToniMorrisonHomePage.<http://www.luminarium.com>.
17. Toni Morrison. Love. New York: Plume, 2003. 1.
18. Wilfred D. Samuels, and Clenora Hudson-Weems. Toni Morrison. New York: Twayne, 1990. 97. All subsequent references indicated parenthetically are to this book.

QUEST FOR BLUE EYES IN THE BLUEST EYE

Beauty is said to be in the eyes of the beholder, but what if the image of beauty is forced into the minds of many? The beauty of a person could be expressed in many different ways, as far as looks and personality goes, but the novel The Bluest Eye begs to differ. It contradicts the principle, because beauty is no longer just a person's opinion but beauty has been made into an unwritten rule, a standard made by society for society. The most important rule is that in order to be beautiful, girls have to look just like a white doll, with blue eyes, light pink skin, and have blond hair. And if they're not, they are not beautiful. W.E.B DuBois, in his book, The Souls of Black Folk gauges the deleterious impact of racism on cultural self-consciousness and identity. The term, "double-consciousness", refers to two distinct realities-a psychological conflict between opposing cultural world views and debilitating resolution in which externally derived and distorted perceptions of the self constitute a single, but alienated self-consciousness. DuBois further notes: "It is a peculiar sensation, this double-consciousness, this sense of always looking at one's self through the eyes of others, of measuring one's soul by the tape of a world that looks on in amused contempt and pity."[1]

Jane Rosenmary Clay (1963:11), one of the Afro-American poets, writes:

> You [America] are my country... but you do not want me.
> You have belittled and degraded me until I have become
> little and degraded. You have not believed in me, until I no
> longer believe in myself. You have not accepted me, until I
> no longer accept myself. [2]

Toni Morrison in her piece of fiction, titled, The Bluest Eye catches the gnawing self-consciousness, bashfulness and reticence of an innocent black girl. Pecola has recently stepped into the world where perceptions are made by looking at one's outer physical reality. Bewildered at being labelled misfit, Pecola endeavours to be akin to the social world around her. Thus, begins her quest, a pursuit to achieve the existing American standards of beauty-blue eyes, blond hair and white skin. Since this desire is not feasible, she suffers from the pangs of being unworthy, unwanted and undesired. Pecola's yearning for blue eyes is an external manifestation of the internal need to be loved and accepted by the white community.

> Pecola Breedlove is a young black girl driven literally
> insane by the pressure toward absolute physical beauty in
> a culture whose white standards of beauty… are impossible
> for her to meet, though no less alluring and
> demanding. Surrounded by cultural messages that she is
> ugly by definition, she can achieve peace only by retreating
> into schizophrenia. [3]

Pecola who never considers herself beautiful, is all admiration for the eyes of the whites which she longs to possess through some miracle. Her obsession with physical beauty leads to disastrous consequences. And as Morrison herself states, "the concept of physical beauty as a virtue is one of the dumbest, most pernicious and destructive ideas of the western world." [4]

Pigeonholed to be one of community's ugly children, Pecola lives life each day wanting to be accepted. The wider community also fails Pecola. Having absorbed the idea that she is ugly and knowing that she is unloved; Pecola desperately wants the blue eyes that she understands will make a child lovable in American society.

> The attempt to become "white" intensifies rather
> than mitigates the Negro woman's frustration in white
> world. No amount of pain, powder and hair straightner
> can erase all things in the black woman's background
> that make her feminity and aesthetic appearance of
> herself as beauty capable of attracting men. The Negro
> woman becomes ashamed of what she is… [5]

As a black girl, Pecola undergoes all the traumatic experiences. She wants to rise up out of the pit of her blackness and see that world with blue eyes, but the pity is that she is not allowed to. Excluded from reality by inequality and discrimination, she goes mad. Fantasizing that her eyes have turned blue and so fitted her for the world.

While tracking the novel from a humanistic angle one is stumped by the bareness and infertility that has cropped up in human associations. The society is not ready to accept a child because she doesn't conform to the regularized standards of beauty. The society allows the weight of ugliness to burden the innocent mind of Pecola. No polite words, no loving hands, no warm bosoms are lent to this poor black girl. The unspoken words, worries and pains of Pecola remain unapprehended. She is just another unwanted, unworthy being, churned in the mechanical cycle of this world. It is the dehumanizing society that engenders a colonial situation, sustains it through excessively violent means, destroys the victim both physically and psychologically, and finally, leaves him into pathetic state of powerlessness and psychic impotency. Selwyn R. Cudjoe (1984:14) critiques:

> …the major crime of the society is that it attempts to
> reduce all Negroes to a sense of impotence and
> nothingness. [6]

Moreover, the oppressive system operates by seducing, pressuring, or forcing the victim or the members of the subordinate groups to replace individual and cultural ways of knowing with the dominant group's 'special' thoughts. Subtle but highly pervasive manifestations of socialization or indoctrination operate in all ramifications and finally lead the alleged to believe in their inferiority. The primer, which talks about economic disparities, also refers to the portrayal of what the whites reject-blackness, overt sexuality, lack of cleanliness and insubordination. The primer represents cultural colonization and repression of any deviant attribute. This is what every student reads in the first lesson in the first school. There, pictures of Dick, Jane, father, mother, the cat and the dog are drilled powerfully into young minds. Words have power; pictures have power. Blue eyes, blond hair, fair skin are the symbols of beauty valued in the west as proclaimed by romantic movies, bill-boards, and the reaction of people of golden objects. The violence inherent in this perspective is that only white is beautiful. Beauty exists in and of itself, independent of human nature or character, human beings are considered unequal and superior or inferior according to their nearness yardstick. As Cynthia A. Davies points out, "Pecola is the epitome of the victim in a world that reduces persons to objects and then makes them feel inferior as objects." [7]

Morrison depicts Pecola as a victim of an evil that has roots deeper than human conviction and can't be understood in such terms. This vicious cycle of rejection, this embodiment of supernatural forces of the creator, creation, and the created combine to produce the evil that left Pecola Breedlove barren and unable to

20

know how or why. Toni Morrison attempts to satisfy this more difficult question of why. Although unspoken, this question obsessively hovers over Pecola throughout the novel and in her circular narrative style Morrison weaves a story that seeks to answer this question by gathering all of the forces that were instrumental in the creation of a social mishap. By using what seem like tangents in the story, we are shown examples of how forces beyond human control such as nature, an omniscient being and primarily a legacy of rejection have joined hands with human insensitiveness to establish the heritage of desolation that has been passed on to Pecola Breedlove.

A child is a progeny of his parents. The beliefs, ideologies and dogmas that find home in their minds are transmitted through their blood to their children. Pecola's belief of her own ugliness is a disease, roots of which can be found in her mother Pauline and Cholly Breedlove. The Breedloves despise themselves because they believe in their own unworthiness which is translated into ugliness for the woman of the family.

> It was as though some mysterious all knowing master
> has given each one a cloak of ugliness to wear, and they
> had each accepted it without question. [8] (28)

Pauline, who works as a domestic servant in a beautiful house, hates the ugliness of her house, her daughter, her family and herself. She lavishes all her love and affection on her employer's daughter, reserving her jibes and slaps for her hapless daughter. In her master's house Pecola's nervous carelessness is given harsh rebuttal while the little girl in pink is greeted with warm apologies and assurances. When the little girl seeks introduction of the visitors, she goes to the extent of describing her own flesh and blood as "none" (85). The tendency of the black people to harass other black-people is a direct indictment of self-loathing, a legacy of white hegemony. White standards corrupted the minds of black people in such a way that black people have developed self-hatred:

> The masters had said, "you are ugly people." They looked
> about themselves and saw nothing to contradict
> the statement, saw in fact, support for it leaning at them
> from every billboard, every move, every glance. (28)

Pauline has been over the years brought into the folds of the society. She has learnt that it is not possible to fight the racist system and has made peace with it. Working in a white man's house, being a demi-mother to the white child, at least gives her a sense of worthiness. She is allowed to live in her dream house and forget for a while her alienation from the society. These blacks were cultural half-breeds, half saxonized, unassimilated, marginal, whose culture was substituted by the most rudimentary American culture of the cheap newspaper, the movies, the popular song, the ubiquitous automobile. Moved by English shibboleths and prejudice "the fear of stranger", these aggressive and frustrated men developed personality needs and psychological strength by scapegoating and stereotyping the blacks. They colonized their very thoughts with their ideas and made the subjugated blacks conform to their terms of structuralization. "This constituted the core of American culture and enabled the white elite to maintain its super-ordinate position politically, economically and socially over the centuries."[9] Any deviation from the entrenched inflexible social system led to negativism and backlash.

Carter G. Woodson (1969: xxxiii), a great Afro-American political thinker and activist argues:

> When 'the Negro's mind has been brought under the
> control of his oppressor, the problem of holding the
> Negro down is easily solved. When you control man's
> thinking, you do not have to tell him not to stand here or
> go yonder. [10]

Pauline Breedlove's personal history is shown to have played out in extreme measures in the life of her daughter. From the early part of her life up to the time the reader is introduced to Pauline, she has worn a shroud of shame. The novel says that it is due primarily to her injured foot that she felt a sense of separateness and unworthiness and also why she "never felt at home anywhere, or that she belonged anyplace" (111). This feeling was intensified by her experiences of exclusion and loneliness after moving up north. She was confronted by prejudice on a daily basis, both classicism and racism, and for the first time, the white standard of beauty. These experiences worked to transform Pauline into a product of hatred and ignorance, leading her to hold herself up to standards that she didn't fully understand nor could realistically attain. These standards and feelings of rejection are the qualities that Pecola inherits from Pauline. Her mother, from her birth, placed upon her the same shroud of shame, loneliness, and inadequacy. More significantly, just as in the Whitcomb dynasty, the Breedloves as a whole are at one point described by the narrator as one distressing unit. They are unified in their acceptance of the mantle of unexplained ugliness, shame, and social dysfunctionality. The narrator tells us that

> No one could have convinced them that they were not
> relentlessly and aggressively ugly...You looked at them
> and wondered why they were so ugly; you looked closely
> and could not find the source. Then you realized that it came
> from conviction, their conviction...And they took the ugliness
> in their hands, threw it as a mantle over them, and went
> about the world with it. Dealing with it each according to his
> own way. (39)

Cholly and Pauline Breedlove came to the city after leading a life of unfathomable penury and deprivation in the southern plantations. But in the city they do not achieve their aim of leading a good, comfortable and secure life. Although free and equal to whites legally, they realize that any semblance of happiness is illusory. The Bluest Eye opens with the Dick - Jane primer:

> Here is the house. It is green and white. It has a red door.
> It is very pretty. Here is the family. Mother, Father, Dick and
> Jane live in the green and white house. They are very happy.
> See Jane. She has a red dress. She wants to play. Who will
> play with Jane. See the cat. It goes meow-meow. Come and
> play. Come play with Jane. The kitten will not play. See
> mother. Mother is very nice. Mother, will you play with
> Jane? Mother laughs. Laugh mother laugh. See father. He is
> big and strong. Father is smiling, Smile. Father, smile. See
> the dog. Bowwow goes the dog. Do you want to play
> with Jane? See the dog run. Run, dog run. Look. Look.
> Here comes a friend. The friend will play with Jane. They
> will play a good game. Play, Jane, play. (7)

This primer is the very epitome of the cultural violence inflicted upon the black race for centuries. The picture is that of a white family with a beautiful home and maximum economic achievement - a picture of an ideal family, The very fact that Jane plays only with her father, mother, cat or dog, shows that contact with other children especially blacks is negative and conflict ridden, resulting in high levels of human concerns. The picture reeks with capitalistic, materialist designs and ideological belief of the hegemonic whites. It is a picture of the white majority that subordinates the black race as well as other immigrants in America. The blacks, being the lowliest in the social hierarchy are first in the line of attack. This is an ideal family set-up, and therefore cannot be but of a white family. Blacks cannot and do not have such pretty houses and almost an idyllic life pattern of security and comfort. A black home is characterized by absent or violent fathers and poverty- ridden mothers whose quest for survival of the family leaves them with no time for 'playing with Janes'. The picture of the ironically titled Breedlove household is a stark contrast to this Edenic primer. Its harsh juxtaposition is suggestive of the blatant core reality of black economic structure:

> There is an abandoned store on the southeast corner
> of Broadway and Thirty-Fifth Street in Lorraine, Ohio. It
> doesn't recede into its background of leaven sky nor
> harmonize with the gray frame houses and black telephone
> poles around it. Rather it foists itself on the eye of
> the passerby in a manner that is both irritating
> and melancholy. Visitors who drive to this tiny town
> wonder why it has not been torn down, while pedestrians,
> who are residents of the neighborhood, simply look away
> when they pass it (30).

Again, for instance, the house of Claudia McTeers, the black girl narrator of the story, is in a dilapidated condition. Claudia says; "our house is old, cold, and green. At night a kerosene lamp lights one large room. The others are traced in darkness, peopled by roaches and mites".(5) The white hegemonic elite, whose characteristics are whiteness and purity, individualism, materialism, economic development, a sense of 'manifest destiny' are all brought to the fore in the primer. The primer, like the rest of the novel <u>The Bluest-Eye</u>, is a manifestation of the true colors of the

24

Anglo-Saxon majority who came to America with a materialistic and exploitative vision. The primer becomes an index to the utter bleakness and aridity permeating black families, which are torn apart due to economic upheavals primarily.

Despite all efforts to give meaning to their lives, to satisfy their cravings to have a house as described in the 'Dick-Jane primer'; Cholly could only manage a low paid job in the factory. Such incredulously low salaries could only give him an old, dingy, squalid 'store front', where they could just fester together - like an ugly, putative Sore - in the debris of a realtors whim. Devoid of material appurtenances, sapped of all zeal and vigor:

> They [jus'l slipped in and out of the box of peeling gray
> making no stir in the neighborhood, no sound in the labor
> force and no wave in the mayor's office. Each   member of
> the family in his own cell of consciousness, each
> making his own patch work, quilt of reality-collecting fragments of
> experience here, pieces of information there.
> For the tiny impressions gleaned from one another,
> they created a sense of belonging and tried to make do
> with the way they found each other (25).

The juxtaposition of the Dick-Jane primer with the old, dilapidated storefront of the Breedlove family points to another major aspect of racial discrimination wherein housing becomes the chief external badge of inferiority. The Breedloves live in battered, tottering old, squalid, dingy house abandoned by whites, instead of newly developed neighborhoods and housing, where the conditions are unduly shameful and oppressive. They live a grossly circumscribed life. They lead oppressive lives in the South, but at least they had the grass and trees and open spaces that reinvigorated them, but in these ghettos of the north, sans all these facilities, they live and die like rodents, pests and insects. The whites have systematically not opened up their great white noose around the urban center cities, to an appreciable extent. Such squalid conditions, the result of blatant exploitation, can only produce neurosis and disintegration. It was prejudice, which is responsible for the concentration of the Negroes in the ghettoes - a consequence of the general pattern of social exclusion of Negroes from the mainstream of American life. "Fear of white people, poverty, and lack of social contacts is factors responsible for their ghettoized existence." [11]

Such conditions, the results of white discrimination made life hell for the black families. The sorry state of affairs was not simply an urban phenomenon, but it persisted in the rural South too. We get a fair idea of the strangulating noose of economic deprivation in the childhood of Cholly. Economic reasons made Cholly's father abandon his mother who then is left with no alternative but to dump Cholly in a garbage box. His abandoned and destitute aunt, luckily or unluckily, rescues Cholly. The struggle to survive begins. When Cholly is twelve years old, his aunt dies. The following conversation at her funeral, conveys effectively her deprived status, where the rules framed keeping in mind the white middle class family set-up, do nothing to aid a forlorn and old, abandoned wretch like her:

> I'll say. Did she leave anything?
> Not even a pocket-handkerchief. The house belongs
> to some white folks In Clarksvllle.
> Oh, yeah? I thought she owned it.
> May have at one time. But not no more I hear the
> insurance folks been down talking to her brother.
> How much do it come?
> Eighty-five dollars. I hear. That all?
> Can she get in the ground on that?
> Don't see how...
> Seems a shame. She been paying on that insurance all
> her life. (111)

Pauline's relation with her husband Cholly is also not amiable. They pick fight with each other for the gratification of their existence. It gave meaning and substance to their dull, tiny, undistinguishable days. Their fight for power in the household is an outcome of their failed positions in society. The latter wouldn't provide them an essence before existence, so they try to achieve it at least in their household.

> To deprive her of all the zest and reasonableness of
> life. Cholly, by his habitual drunkenness and
> orneriness, provided them both with the material they
> needed to make their lives tolerable. (31)

Pauline could make her life worthwhile by working on the traditions set by society. The society had lowered her self-esteem by branding her ugly and unworthy. She would do the same with Cholly to rule in her home. His heedlessness, carelessness gave her a position of authority. Seen in comparison to him she was then to be proven better.

> Get him, Jesus! Get him!" If Cholly had stopped drinking, she
> would never have forgiven Jesus. She needed Cholly's
> sins desperately. The lower he sank, the wilder and
> more irresponsible he became, the more splendid she and her
> task became. (31)

Pecola's parents, furthermore, are often powerless themselves, subject to the whites who employ them, victims of their poverty and the culture which invalidates them.

Only a good, steady job, an adequate and dependable income can lend stability to a family. Absence of a good economic base leads to quarrels and ultimately break-up. The function of family stability required by society and desired by family members is impossible unless the economic functions of the family are fulfilled.[12] Cholly is unable to perform the instrumental functions like providing for the education and health of his family effectively, because of rigid and in built discrimination. The white breadwinner's security of employment is denied to Negro breadwinners like Cholly and these economic deprivations have a direct bearing on the performance of the father in performing instrumental duties.[13] The inability to perform these duties necessarily hampers 'psychic security 'and the mental health of the family. Cholly is unable to provide the kind of atmosphere that can galvanize his family into a close-knit unit exuding self-worth, self-awareness, dignity, companionship and a sense of belonging. Less income strains family life and impairs the instrumental functions of the family. It, thereby, adversely affects the more expressive functional relationship in the family.

> Cholly and me were getting along good then. We came up
> north; supposed to be more jobs and all. We moved into
> two rooms up over a furniture store and I set about house
> keeping. Cholly was working at the steel plant, and
> everything was looking good. I don't know what all
> happened. Everything changed. (91)

Cholly and Pauline had less and still less money. Consequently, after the birth of children the desperation increased. Helpless and without adequate means of survival their married life was in tatters and Cholly grew violent. There was no love and harmony in their relationship. In their struggle for survival they fought ceaselessly. Cholly, unable to fight against the hegemonic white system, begins to do what the whites had been doing all along. He begins oppressing his doubly oppressed folk even more. It was the peculiar historical development, which promoted the caste like qualities in the American stratification, which reduced Negroes like Cholly to utter deprivation. Such dehumanizing poverty made men like Cholly into animals from the loving human beings that they were.[14] The socio-economic instability affected not only his wife but also his children especially Pecola, his young daughter. It is within the family that child develops his personality, intelligence aspiration and, indeed, his moral character. "The socialization of the child therefore becomes the most exclusive domain of the family, but all these qualities can flower only in a house where there is economic stability."[15] Pecola is born in a family, a colored family, which is not evil or bad but which is definitely not rich. It is her family's poverty, which becomes its greatest sin. Black and poor, the family is condemned as evil and bad. So, seemingly out of hate, but actually due to abominable poverty, "Cholly and Mrs. Breedlove [Pauline] fought each other with darkly brutal formalism" (37).

The children felt throttled by the violent relationship of their parents. Unable to bear it any longer the son Sammy runs away by the time he was fourteen. The daughter restricted by youth and sex could do little other than passively endure the excruciating agony. "She struggled between an overwhelming desire that one would kill the other and a profound wish that she herself would die" (38). In addition, they themselves have been physically or emotionally abandoned by their families- Cholly was rejected by both of his parents; Pauline was made an outsider because of a limp. Traumatized children themselves, they continue the trauma by denying their own weakness in their abuse of parental power, by instilling their own fears of impotence, and by calling upon their children to fulfill their own unmet needs.

The Breedlove's daughter, Pecola, is especially sensitive to the fearful, repetitively ritualized violence that her parents direct toward each other and their children. In this context Pecola becomes especially vulnerable to the sudden, violent traumas of being beaten and rejected by her mother Pauline, and by the more horrific traumas of being raped by her father Cholly and then losing the baby.

28

During one of the fights ensued between her parents she whispers:

> "Please, God," she whispered into the palm of her hand.
> "Please make me disappear." She squeezed her eyes
> shut. Little parts of her body faded away. Now slowly …
> only her tight, tight eyes were left. They were always
> left. (33)

Her eyes would never fail to register the effect the surroundings had on her. Under the oppressive condition, her enslaved self undergoes pathetic diminution and reduction to such an extent that it remains on the verge of extinction. Rollo May asserts:

> With unconscious purpose we close our eyes to reality
> and persuade ourselves that we have escaped it. This kind
> of innocence doesn't make things bright and clear, … it only
> makes them simple and easy… It is this innocence that
> cannot come to terms with the destructiveness in one's self
> and other's…[16]

Never valued as an individual when she was a child, Pauline continues throughout her life to seek approval in others' eyes, particularly in her position as a servant for whites. In the one place that she feels powerful-- the kitchen of the white family for whom she works-- she attacks her daughter (who has spilled a cobbler), and in turn denies her own place in the world when she not only fails to acknowledge Pecola but also comforts the white family's child. Pecola's desire for blue eyes is in fact an inheritance from Pauline herself; based on idealized white images- images of acceptance and beauty completely disconnected from herself and her blackness- Pauline's desire is to look like Jean Harlow. Pauline and Pecola, like the rest of the black community, have internalized the pervasive standard of whiteness: in the white dolls they buy their children, in the movies they watch and emulate, and in their privileging of the light-skinned black child, Maureen Peal, over the darker children. Even through narrative, in the use of the school primer as a structuring device, Morrison has foregrounded the way that their lives are "contained within the framework of the values of the dominant culture and subjected to those values" (21). More subtly, she uses the motif of trauma to suggest the overwhelming power that the larger white culture wields in its slow, relentless obliteration of the value of blackness, which forces them to affirm the dominant perspective because cultivating awareness of their own collusion would bring incredible pain, no readily available form of action, and increased hopelessness.

Cholly's traumatized past ultimately leads to consequences that are even more devastating for his daughter. After being abandoned by his parents, the most formatively brutalizing incident in Cholly's youth was the interruption of his first sexual encounter by armed whites. The experience of being forced by the white hunters to continue relations with his partner constitutes a trauma not only in its humiliating intensity, but also in the impossibility of his being able to react to the situation. The displacement of his anger onto his fellow victim Darlene, as Gibson notes (28), reveals the extent and depth of his psychic wound: "Never did he once consider directing his hatred toward the hunters. Such an emotion would have destroyed him. They were big, white, armed men. He was small, black, helpless." (119). Cholly, in short, cannot assimilate the truth of his subjugation without being annihilated by a sense of his own powerlessness. When the environment sustains him, i.e., when his marriage and work are stable, Cholly copes well, but when these sources of support and stability are taken away his past returns to plague his present actions. Psychological research indicates that stress causes state dependent returns to earlier behavior patterns. A stressful situation will cause thoughts to travel along the same pathways as those connected to a previous traumatic event, and if immediate stimuli recall this event, the individual will be transported back to that somatic (bodily) state and react accordingly; responding as if faced with past threat, and losing the mental synthesis that constitutes reflective will and belief, the individual will simply transform into automatic wills and beliefs the impulses which are momentarily the strongest. Such is the process which accounts in part for Cholly's rape of Pecola.

When Pecola makes a gesture which reminds him of the tender feelings he once had for Pauline, Pecola's sadness and helplessness and his own inability to make her happy provoke a repetition of the violent impotence and the helpless fear that he and Darlene felt with the white men. His angry response toward Darlene returns and becomes confounded with feelings of love for Pauline and Pecola, and also with self hatred, because Pecola is like Cholly once was, small and impotent. His pessimistic attitudes toward life, himself and his capacity to love return to this traumatic context, and he loses the ability to approach life or his daughter positively. One way for him to rid himself of his fears is to project them onto Pecola, and in part he tries to destroy those fears by raping her. Bertha M. Williams (1974:204)[17] describes such persons as "inhibitory personalities." They become derivative personalities because they cannot validate their own self-esteem, self-worth, or self-importance in their own terms.

Cholly's unnatural rape of Pecola could be interpreted "as a pathetic attempt to return to the heady days of first love when his very presence essentially created another human being. Cholly turns to Pecola in hopes of rescuing her from the dehumanizing glare of all white people and a subsequent loveless existence. His tenderness and protectiveness, however, unfortunately slip into lust and rag which he directs at Pecola and all those like her who bore witness to his failure, his impotence, the one whom he had not been able to protect, to spare, to cover from the round moon glow of the flashlight. It is, thus, the distortion of his love for Pecola. The latter's still-born child is not only a symbol of his personal violation but of the fettered life she has been made to live. This type of projection as a manifestation of the trauma victim's dissociation from the truth of his or her situation is not unique to Cholly. The community in which the Breedlove family lives also projects its own sense of devaluation onto the Breedloves, dismissing them for being "low," ugly outsiders, when actually they are merely extreme examples of the larger group's own abasement by white culture. An important example of this projection may be seen in the way that another member of their community, Geraldine, separates herself from "trashy" blacks like Pecola, who she believes threaten her position vis a vis whites.

> She looked at Pecola, Saw the dirty torn dress, the plaits
> sticking out on her head, hair matted where the plaits
> had come undone, the muddy shoes with the wad of
> gum peeping out from between the cheap soles....She
> had seen this little girl all of her life....[children like
> Pecola] crowded into pews at church, taking space from
> the nice, neat colored children....Like flies they hovered;
> like flies they settled. And this one had settled in her
> house. (75)

In her poverty and blackness, Pecola represents everything that Geraldine is "fighting to suppress," and in telling Pecola to leave her house she is "attempting to rid herself of her fears of her own unworthiness, of her own shadow of blackness."[18] Geraldine's disregard of Pecola represents what Donald Gibson sees as Morrison's acknowledgment of the black community's participation in its own oppression (21). Geraldine and others fail to recognize that they are outsiders in a white world. Not recognizing that they themselves are what Morrison calls a "pariah community," they reject and revile their own members, like the Breedloves, whereas they should examine the condition of such detested members as useful for the realistic evaluation their own community's subjugation.

People like Geraldine chose to call themselves 'colored', a word variedly different from black. These girls perfectly jacketed the contours and frameworks of ideal beings specified by the society:

> These sugar-brown Mobile girls move through the
> Streets without a stir. They are as sweet and plain
> as buttercake. Slim ankles; long, narrow feet. They
> wash themselves with orange-colored Lifebuoy soap,
> dust themselves with Cashmere Bouquet talc… They go to
> land grant colleges, normal schools, and learn how to do
> the white man's work with refinement… (64)

In fact, these girls were a replica of white girls, differing only in their color. Geraldine seemed to carry the flag for this race. Her son Junior was forbidden to do anything with black children. She had explained to him the difference between colored people and niggers.

> Colored people were neat and quiet; niggers were dirty
> and loud. He belonged to the former group…The line
> between colored and nigger was not always clear; subtle
> and telltale signs threatened to erode it, and the watch
> had to be constant. (67)

Junior used to long to play with black boys, however, under the weight of his mother's cultural dilemma, his desires found no room. Mary Daly[19] believes that the oppressive society not only seeks to dehumanize the enslaved persons but even attempts to wipe out their traditions and consciousness. Moreover, it operates by seducing, pressuring, or forcing the, members of the subordinated class to replace individual and cultural ways of knowing with the dominant group's 'special thoughts'. As a result the victim is left with a suspended culture that is subject to change according to the whim and fancies of the society. Geraldine is living a mechanical life, satisfying all the physical needs of the family. With respect to the needs of the soul, there arises no particular thought. Pecola when forced to enter the haven of Geraldine is overwhelmed by its immense grandeur. However, her entry into this new world is marred by her introduction to the cruel workings of the human mind. Junior treats her like an object to be used for his benefit. She is insulted and thrown out to show her right place in the social order. Geraldine, a black woman who is said to have suppressed her racial identity by getting rid of "the dreadful funkiness of passion, the funkiness of nature, the funkiness of the wide range of human emotions" in order to appease the white man's "blunted soul" (68), treats Pecola as not only a nuisance or blight, but as a threat to the "sanitized" - i.e., anti-black - environment that she has constructed around her son. As Pecola is thrown out of Geraldine's house, she sees a portrait of an Anglicized Jesus "looking down at her with sad and unsurprised eyes" (72), an image of a God who seems either incapable of helping her or complicit in her suffering.

The Breedlove family, the epitome of this devalued community, suffers from trauma caused by single and startling events, in the form of daily, grinding oppression, whereby the parents pass their suffering on to their children. Her further devaluation by the world, with little relief except from her playmates and the whores who befriend her, includes constant ridicule from other school children because of her dark skin, poverty and ugliness. The black boys who torment her fail to recognize a fellow member of their community. As Michael Awkward observes, their insults ironically reflect "their ability to disregard their similarity to their victim; the verse they compose to belittle her ('Black e mo...Yadaddsleepsnekked') reflects their own skin color and, quite possibly, familial situations."[20] White attitudes toward blacks are exemplified in Pecola's encounter with the storeowner, Mr. Yacobowski:

> She looks up at him and sees the vacuum where
> curiosity ought to lodge. And something more. The
> total absence of human recognition- the glazed
> separateness" (36).

Further, Morrison writes:

> All things in her are flux with anticipation. But, her
> blackness is static and dread. And it is this blackness
> that accounts for, that creates the vacuum edge with
> distaste in white eyes (37).

In the encounter between Pecola and Yacobawaski, latter's petrifying look assumes great symbolic significance. Like Medusa's look, which was capable of turning people to stone, Yacobowski's look devastates Pecola. His 'look ' suggests that a black girl like Pecola does not exist. For whites like Yacobowski, she is and will always remain invisible.

> Sartre posits 'hat the awareness of being seen is not only
> a way of affirming the existence of the other but
> of understanding the dynamic of the relationship with
> the other. One way that I affirm the existence of the
> other, Sartre argues, is through the 'Look'.[22]

As Hazel. E. Barnes, explains, Yacobowsky's 'look' psychologically annihilates Pecola, by ignoring her free subjectivity. She is reduced to the status of thing in the world. It reveals her physical and psychic vulnerability, and her fragility. Pecola whom we meet before the encounter with Yacobowski lacks a sense of place. She has been abandoned by her family. Consequently, she becomes a 'case' i.e., a ward of the country without any place of residence. In fact, we learn that because of the fragmentation of the Breedlove family, Pecola has been put outdoors. Thus, Pecola's essential invisibility symbolizes her status as an object within the community and her family. Hence she is already and totally alienated. The encounter with Yacobowski, aggravates her self-hatred. She is already suffering from a negative self-concept. At the moment she encounters Yacobawaski's blue eyes, Pecola exits the sanctuary of her thoughts. Whatever little confidence she might be having is completely destroyed. She enters the open battlefield that market becomes. Ironically, the shopkeeper feels "he does not need to waste the effort of a glance" (36). His 'look' implies that for him, there is "nothing (no thing) to see" (36). His glance achieves its purpose of identifying and negatives the 'object' perceived. Pecola interprets his action as signifying distaste for her blackness. Pecola who is deeply affected by the dominant norms of beauty and desires blue eyes blond hair and pink skin and hates at the same time her black skin and kinky hair. Her sense of shame when she encounters Yacobowski's 'look" reveals that she imbibes the significance it conveys, not only for him but for all whites. (Weems17-18)

Consequently she equates herself with the dandelion weeds she passes by. Pecola is reduced to a state of complete worthlessness due to the neutralizing and petrifying effect of Yacobowski's 'look'. The total absence of human recognition that Pecola sees in Yacobawski's glance corresponds to her own negative self-perception. She is reduced to a state of thing hood, a 'being- for-the- other.' Pecola responds only with shame and allows herself to be defined by the 'other'(Weems18-19). She could easily have chosen anger, for "anger stirs and wakes in her; it opens its mouth and like the hot mouthed puppy, laps up the dredges of her shame" (37). In one of the few places where the author seems to intrude to admonish, we are told: "anger is better. There is a sense of being' in anger', a reality and presence, an awareness of worth. It is a lovely surging" (37-38). But rather than choosing this creative act Pecola acquiesces and, thus, is consumed by shame:

> "This anger will not hold; the puppy is too easily surfeited.
> Its thirst too quickly quenched, it sleeps. The shame wells
> up again, its muddy rivulet seeping into her eyes. What to
> do before the tears come. She remembers the
> Mary-Janes". (38)

Whites, or the whole hegemonic society, therefore, have very effectively and durably mobilized their institutions to buttress and reproduce their culture. They have entrenched an arsenal of sexual and racial authority every where. They have managed to exclude the real world. No woman or man of color has been able to discover the representation of her/his cultural voice. They have created an order wherein blacks are subjugated, made voiceless, invisible, underrepresented and of-course unrepresentable. The western male subject has long been constituted historically for himself and in himself. Blacks were denied and are still being denied the process of exploring and reclaiming their subjectivity.

Though not specifically addressing trauma, many critics of Morrison's work, in particular Cynthia A. Davis, analyze how oppression is represented in the form of "psychic violence," i.e., the destructiveness of a white racist society which is not always physically brutal, but destroys by engaging in "the systematic denial of the reality of black lives"[22]. Roberta Rubenstein also sees Morrison's work as illustrating that the "constriction of the growth of the self is implicitly linked to restrictive or oppressive cultural circumstances"[23]. The role of scapegoat which is assigned to the abused child Pecola in The Bluest Eye reveals the connection between her devastated life and those of the other individuals in her community. Not psychically able to acknowledge their own lack of power, their seeming lack of sympathy with Pecola is really a displacement "onto the Other all that is feared in the self."[24] To avoid a sense of their own victimization, the community projects its sense of inferiority onto Pecola, who is the quintessence of the victim in a world that reduces persons to objects, thus diluting their entire existence; in order to escape from a similar fate their response is to act within "the interlocking hierarchies that allow most to feel superior to someone."[25]

This cycle of rejection is developed further in the metaphors that Morrison uses throughout the novel. One such metaphor can be seen in Pecola's perception of the dandelion and how it mirrors her perception of herself. In one scene Pecola passes a patch of dandelions as she walks into Mr. Yacobowski's store. "Why, she wonders, do people call them weeds? She thought they were pretty" (35). Yet after suffering the embarrassment of Mr. Yacobowski's vacuous, shame inducing stare the faint glimmer of happiness she experiences in seeing the dandelion is destroyed. When she leaves and passes the dandelions again she thinks, "They are ugly. They are weeds" (37). She has transferred society's dislike of her to the dandelions and it is not until the end of the novel that Morrison fully explains these metaphors. Through an adult Claudia, Morrison says, "I even think now that the land of the entire country was hostile to marigolds that year. Certain seeds it will not nurture, certain fruits it will not bear and when the land kills of its own volition, we say that the victim had no right to live" (164). Even nature retains the right to dictate which seeds it will bear to fruition and those that it will reject. Pecola is one of these "certain seeds" that never had a chance to grow and succeed because she lived in an environment that rejected her, one that would not and maybe could not nurture her.

Morrison does not stop at the forces of nature or "genealogy" but she also places a responsibility for this social dilemma on an ambiguous god and/or the church. This omniscient being, the creator of all things, both noble and corrupt, and his messengers have in a sense sanctioned the unfavorable in order to validate the hatred and scorn of the "righteous." In her introduction to the Breedlove family, Morrison impugns the Breedlove's acceptance of ugliness to a higher power saying, "It was as though some mysterious all-knowing master had given each one a cloak of ugliness to wear" (28). This divine being not only created ugliness for them but it also ambiguously created an environment that rejected and scorned this ugliness. In her youth Pauline struggles with the same type of ambiguity and contradiction in trying to "hold her mind on the wages of sin," while "her body trembled for redemption, salvation and a mysterious rebirth that would simply happen, with no effort on her part" (113).

Ironically, at the end of the novel it is Soaphead Church, an individual well acquainted with theology, who alone posits an answer to Claudia's initial question of why. His letter, addressed to "HE who greatly ennobled human nature by creating it," intends to familiarize an omniscient being with the "facts which have either escaped HIS notice, or which HE has chosen to ignore" (140) saying that God forgot about the children.

> "You said, 'Suffer the little children to come unto me,
> and harm them not.' Did you forget? Did you forget about
> the children? Yes. You forgot. You let them go wanting,
> sitting on road shoulders, crying next to their dead
> mothers. I've seen them charred, lame, halt. You forgot,
> Lord. You forgot how and when to be God...That's why
> I changed the little black girl's eyes for her...I did what
> You could not do. I looked at that ugly little black girl and
> I loved her. I played You". (144)

This letter not only incriminates God but it also incriminates the church. In their duty to come to the aid of the despised and dejected they have failed and instead begun to play God themselves, judging society's mistakes in the name of righteous superiority. This is evident in Soaphead's gift of the miraculous and Pauline's successfully achieved martyrdom at the cost of her marriage and the lives of her children. By incriminating God, Morrison questions the very existence of this world. If its harbinger is biased, the world will be topsy-turvy too. Sophead Church's claims of helping Pecola have good intentions but the process of doing it is another evidence of the inhuman practices on which the society runs its devious course. Sophead gave Pecola an illusion of having 'Blue Eyes'.

> "Each night Pecola prayed for blue eyes. In her eleven
> years,no one had ever noticed Pecola. But with blue eyes,
> she thought, everything would be different. She would be
> so pretty that her parents would stop fighting. Her
> father would stop drinking. Her brother would stop
> running away. If only she could be beautiful. If only
> people would look at her." (Back Cover)

This illusion made it easier for her to sustain in the hostile society. Having blue eyes meant being accepted, being a part of the human race. This illusion though, turns her schizophrenic but it is a better proposition in comparison to the heavy weight of nothingness under which she lived earlier.

The primer or the epigraphical introduction reveals the insidious circle of education. Education is designed to oppress the already oppressed still further and at the same time it teaches them to enact self-oppression while ostensibly making them learn to read a simple, unproblematic text. The reading material expresses the values of the dominant culture. Such education exacts a terrible price-the price of alienation from one's own culture, as a payment for the privilege of education. One cannot simply learn to read without being subjected to the values being incorporated through the value-oriented words. Black children like Pecola are taught to read in the very act of reading. Hence they are unconsciously conditioned by a political, religious, moral, ideological aesthetic that is definitely not connected with their actual lives. Standards are fixed using genetics and economics and the black children and of course the adults fall pitiably short of these standards, leading to a cultural mutilation and inferiority complex in the black children. This violence of the education system, together with mass media's negative penetration, coupled with economic and social realities would but naturally create rootlessness, alienation and abnormal spurts of action from the blacks.

It is not unnatural to have or to want blue eyes but white society holds such a standard as the best. It impresses the reality of its value on those not having the wherewithal to resist. It arbitrarily controls images through control of magazines, newspapers, and window signs, which rapture their psyche completely. The blacks do not have the facilities to counter the assault. Pecola, who is assaulted continuously by such ideological definition of beauty, loses her confidence and develops self-contempt. In school her fairer Negro classmates taunt her - "black e mo. black e mo. Ya dad dsleeps naked black e mo black e mo ya dad d sleeps naked. black e mo ..."(55).

The narrator, Claudia, who happens to be Pecola's classmate and friend says that they had extemporized a verse made up of two insults about matters over which the victim had no control: the color of her skin and speculations on the sleeping habits of an adult, widely fitting in its incoherence. The fact that these carriers of social decorum were themselves black or that their own father had similarly relaxed habits was irrelevant. It was their contempt for their own blackness that gave the first insult its teeth. They seemed to have taken all of their cultivated ignorance, their exquisitely learned self-hatred, their elaborately designed hopelessness and sucked it all up into a fiery cone of scorn that had burned for ages in the hollows of their minds - cooled - and spilled over lips of outrage, consuming whatever was in its path. They danced a macabre ballet around the victim, whom, for their own sake they were prepared to sacrifice to the flaming pit (55).

In Ralph Ellison's Invisible Man, the protagonist encounters a sign in a Harlem store window with the following inscription: "you too can be truly beautiful and win greater happiness with whiter complexion. Be outstanding in your social set up".[26]

Toni Morrison is one with Ralph Ellison's views when she writes:

The concept of physical beauty as virtue is one of the
dangerous, most preciousness and destructive ideas of the
western world. Pecola in her depressed, agonized,
helpless state of mind, thinks if those eyes of hers
were different, that is to say, beautiful, she herself would
be different. If she looked different, i.e., beautiful,
maybe Cholly would be different, and Mrs. Breedlove too.[27]

Pecola feels that if she got a pair of blue eyes, may be they'd say, "why look at pretty-eyed Pecola. We mustn't do bad things in front of those pretty eyes"(34). Hence forth this little black girl yearns to have beautiful blue eyes like the little white girls she sees and the horror at the heart of her yearning is exceeded only by the evil of its fulfillment. Like her mother Pauline, Pecola, too falls a victim to the Eurocentric hegemonic discourse and develops self-contempt and complete shattering of confidence. She falls a prey to the ideology that equated mental capacities with color, an ideology which conflates color with intelligence and co-relates blackness with stupidity. In her school, her teachers hardly notice her and make her sit segregated and forlorn on a bench meant for two. In the society at large, she is a victim of the political propaganda of a wholly narrow selfish and vicious nationalism. The political ambition of the whites and their desire for control deliberately fails to reflect the cultural diversity in America. Under the concept of the 'melting pot theory' the whites want to forge a common identity. It is the white identity and white values which eclipses all other cultural identities. There is a complete absence of the already oppressed minorities. Pecola, therefore, is a victim of this political concern (oppression) that colors the so-called inculcation of civic virtues in people.

In sum, Pecola is the central scapegoat of the novel, <u>The Bluest Eye</u>. For she is made an object not only by her parents and mulattos in the novel, but also by the narrator, Claudia, a once caring friend who shuns Pecola in the end. At the end of her assessment, Claudia recognizes Pecola's role as scapegoat:

> All of us-all who knew her-felt so wholesome after we
> cleaned ourselves on her. We were so beautiful when we
> stood astride her ugliness. Her simplicity decorated us, her
> guilt sanctified us, her pain made us glow with health,
> her awkwardness made us think we had a sense of humor.
> Her inarticulateness made us generous. Even her
> waking dreams we used-to silence our own nightmares.
> And she let us, and thereby deserved our contempt. We
> honed our eggs of her, padded our characters with her
> fraility, and yawned in the fantasy of our strength.(163)

Clearly, Claudia maintains that Pecola is equally responsible for the plight she has to suffer. The role in which she is cast is her own doing. Pecola's endeavor to find answer to 'why' leads to her tragic end. As long as one lives passively in this inhuman environment, he is safe. However, the moment pangs of existence attack him, his downfall begins. The inhuman treatment of society has been going on for centuries and may go on too. By questioning it, one may end up being a scapegoat only. Pecola in her quest for blue eyes, in her quest for essence precedes existence, to borrow Sartre's term, has entered the world of schizophrenia. Here, she is happy with her imaginary companion who validates all her desires and gives her an illusion of belongingness. Pecola's desire for blue eyes, while highly unrealistic, is based on one correct insight into her world: she believes that the cruelty she witnesses and experiences is connected to how she is seen. If she had beautiful blue eyes, Pecola imagines, people would not want to do ugly things in front of her or to her. The accuracy of this insight is affirmed by her experience of being teased by the boys— when Maureen comes to her rescue, it seems that they no longer want to behave badly under Maureen's attractive gaze. In a more basic sense, Pecola and her family are mistreated in part because they happen to have black skin. By wishing for blue eyes rather than lighter skin, Pecola indicates that she wishes to see things differently as much as she wishes to be seen differently. She can only receive this wish, in effect, by blinding herself. Pecola is then able to see herself as beautiful, but only at the cost of her ability to see accurately both herself and the world around her. The connection between how one is seen and what one sees has a uniquely tragic outcome for her.

The opening narrative from a Dick-and-Jane reading primer is distorted when Morrison runs its sentences and then its words together. The gap between the idealized, sanitized, upper-middle-class world of Dick and Jane and the often dark and ugly world of the novel is emphasized by the chapter headings excerpted from the primer. But Morrison does not mean for us to think that the Dick-and-Jane world is better—in fact, it is largely because the black characters have internalized white Dick-and-Jane values that they are unhappy. In this way, the Dick and Jane narrative and the novel provide ironic commentary on each other.

Thus, Pecola undergoes all the traumatic experiences, her inheritance from the society. She wants to rise up of the pit of her blackness and see the world with blue eyes, but the pity is that she is not allowed to. Excluded from the world of childhood fantasies, Pecola becomes an object on which the society practices its inhuman tactics. Morrison's purpose of showing us the psychic state and the resultant behavior of Pecola under the pressure of white domination is to expose the vicious genocidal effects of racism on the black girls, thereby raising the larger question of degrading humane perceptions. Racism, feminism comes under the larger fold of humanism. While questioning the former sensibilities in the work of Toni Morrison one is faced with the larger question of the general attitude of society towards the less fortunate ones. It is a tale of twisted, tortured and fractured self's, who yearn for a respectable life of middle class security, in the face of ineradicable and omnipresent economic and racial discrimination. But in the perpetually hostile environment they struggle desperately to survive, to secure the most basic rights against stupendous odds.

The Bluest Eye deals with the moral implication of the state "sponsored ideological biases of beauty and its imprint on young minds and the novel brings into relief the depth and complexity of its implications. Based on experiences, recollections and reminiscences the novel talks about marginal voices and provides a microscopic view of the fallout of such white capitalist ideology that assaults the basic principle of democracy and freedom in America. It denies any basic concept of egalitarian brotherhood and solidarity between the two races in America. The garb of racial or economic discrimination is used to swathe the naked realities of social hostility. The attitude of the whites, mulattoes and others towards Pecola and her lot is in league with the general attitude of the society towards the downtrodden and psychologically weaker beings. The inherent urge, desire, quest of a small girl to be able to imbibe the colors of beauty is an apt example of the dehumanization of the entire human race.

REFERENCES

1. W.E.B. DuBois. The Souls of Black Folk. New York: Avon Books, 1965. 14.
2. Kulkarni, Harihar. Black Feminist Fiction. New Delhi: Creative Books, 1999. 13.
3. Raymond Hedlin. "The Structuring of Emotion in Black American Fiction". Novel: A Forum on Fiction. 16, 1 (1982): 49-50.
4. Toni Morrison. "Behind the Making of The Black Book." Black Book. 23 (1974): 89.
5. William H. Grier and Price M. Cobbs. Black Rage. New York: Basic Books, 1968. xxiii.
6. Selwyn R. Cudjoe. "Maya Angelou and The Autobiographical Statement." In Evans: 6-24.
7. Cynthia Davies. "Self, Society and Myth in Toni Morrison's Fiction." Contemporary Literature. (1982). 23.
8. Toni Morrison. The Bluest Eye. Vintage, 1999. 28. All subsequent references indicated parenthetically are to this text.
9. Sollors Werner. Theories of Ethnicity: a Classical Reader. London: Macmillan, 1996. 95-96.
10. Harihar Kulkarni. Black Feminist Fiction. New Delhi: Creative Books, 1999. 15.
11. Andrew Billingsley. Black Families in White America. New York: A Touchstone Book, 1968. 93.
12. Andrew Billingsley. Black Families in White America. New York: A Touchstone Book, 1968. 24.
13. Andrew Billingsley. Black Families in White America. New York: A Touchstone Book, 1968. 25.
14. Andrew Billingsley. Black Families in White America. New York: A Touchstone Book, 1968. 49.
15. Andrew Billingsley. Black Families in White America. New York: A Touchstone Book, 1968.29.
16. Rollo May. 1972. Power and Innocence: A Search for the Sources of Violence. New York: Dell Publishing, Delta Books. 49.
17. Harihar Kulkarni. Black Feminist Fiction. New Delhi: Creative Books, 1999. 10.

18. Michael Awkward. "The Evil of fulfillment: Scapegoating and Narration in <u>The Bluest Eye</u>". Gates and Appiah, eds., <u>Critical Perspectives.</u> 194.

19. Mary Daly. <u>Beyond God the Father</u>. Boston Beacon Press, 1873. 66.

20. Michael Awkward. "The evil of fulfillment: scapegoat and narration in <u>The Bluest Eye</u>". Gates and Appiah, eds., <u>Critical Perspectives.</u> 191.

21. Wilfred D. Samuels, and Clenora Hudson-Weems. <u>Toni Morrison</u>. New York: Twayne, 1990. 19.

22. Cynthia A. Davies. "Self, Society and Myth in Toni Morrison's Fiction." <u>Journal of Contemporary Literature </u>23. (Summer 1982): 323.

23. Cynthia A. Davies. "Self, Society and Myth in Toni Morrison's Fiction." <u>Journal of Contemporary Literature </u>23. (Summer 1982): 126.

24. Cynthia A. Davies. "Self, Society and Myth in Toni Morrison's Fiction." <u>Journal of Contemporary Literature </u>23. (Summer 1982): 328.

25. Cynthia A. Davies. "Self, Society and Myth in Toni Morrison's Fiction." <u>Journal of Contemporary Literature </u>23. (Summer 1982): 330.

26. Ralph Ellison. <u>The Invisible Man</u>. New York: Penguin Books, 1965. 17.

27. Donald B. Gibson. "Text and Counter text in <u>The Bluest Eye</u>". Ed. Gates and Appiah. <u>Critical Prespectives past and present</u>. New York: Amstead, 1983. 163.

QUEST FOR ABODE IN <u>BELOVED</u>

<u>Beloved</u>, like most black fiction, is about the troubled question of identity and liberty, the agony of social alienation, the longing for a real or, at times, a mythical home. The story focuses on the reappearance of the ghostly character Beloved whose throat was slit open under appalling circumstances eighteen years before, when she was two years old, by her own mother, Sethe. Morrison, through the pages of her fiction brings forth the agony, pain and trepidation of a mother while giving birth to her children in this cruel, inhuman and cold-blooded world. A mother for whom her children is her extension, is ready to cut that chord so that she could save her children from the atrocities which are a part and parcel of this world. It is through the narration of the circumstances leading to her death that the story of Sethe, the central character, and of Paul D and Denver, besides that of other victims of slavery, unfolds before us. It is Beloved's presence that functions as a crypt that hides the truth and meanings of the text. The misery of man in both physical and psychological chains comes forth through the fabric of the novel. <u>Beloved</u> becomes, like the preface which is taken from the biblical book of Hosea, and which reads "I will call them my people which are not my people; and her beloved, which was not beloved."[1] It is a crypt to reveal the past, and conjoin it with their present and future. Toni Morrison uses the primary tool of "memory that creates the chain of tradition, which passes a happening on from generation to generation."[2] Beloved, a crypt, a rememory, helps unfold the catastrophe of history, full of injustices and the unfathomable destruction of the oppressed. <u>Beloved</u> ends in change, a change born in anger and commitment of the oppressed. It is nourished by the image of enslaved ancestors rather than that of liberated grand children.[3] Toni Morrison, through Sethe's rememory of Beloved, halts the progression of the catastrophe. Whenever and wherever possible she tries "to brush history against the grain. In so doing, she shocks the listeners into a critical stance vis-à-vis history."[4] Beloved, becomes a catalyst for revelations as well, as self-revelations, and through her we come to know not only how, but also why, the original child Beloved was killed. And through her also Sethe achieves, finally, her own form of self-exorcism, her own self-accepting peace.[5]

It is the focus on Beloved, then that sets the pace of the novel rolling with Sethe remembering 'Sweet Home':

> ... Suddenly there was sweet home rolling, rolling out
> before her eyes, and although there was not a leaf on
> that farm that did not warn to make her scream, it rolled
> itself out before her in shameless beauty. It never looked
> as terrible as it was and it made her wonder if hell was
> a pretty place too. Fire and brimstone all right, but hidden
> in lacy groves...[6]

This fusion of the images of the past and present in Beloved is designed to break open the continuum of history, to stop the progression which threatened to overwhelm all true experience of the oppressed classes. This fusion is designed "to wrest tradition away from a conformism that is about to overpower it. This fusion shocks the reader into a critical awareness of what has been left out or rendered complete and now must be reclaimed and redeemed."[7] By using multiple voices in Beloved Toni Morrison is able to achieve "that slow piling one on top of the other of thin transparent layers which constitute the most appropriate picture of the way in which the perfect narrative is revealed through the layers of a variety of re-lettings."[8] The characters, in this dense layering of voices, gradually peel away the thin, transparent layers of their stories to reveal the pile of human wreckage wrought by Slavery.

> Beloved is therefore a narrative so punctuated by death
> and brutality, that we are left fixated on the carnage,
> mouth agape, unable to find words to describe what we
> see, and yet longing to awaken the dead and make
> whole what has once been smashed.[9]

Morrison as a history teller through the dialectical image of Beloved, murdered at the mother's hand, breaks the continuity of white history which threatens to bury the slave history. The dialectical image of Beloved fuses the then and the now into a constellation like a flash of lightning. Beloved, as a flesh and blood woman, becomes wholly in the now time of the story. Simultaneously she "brings with her the 'then', the collective memory and the collective rage of the slaves forced from their ancestral homes, piled in ship holds for the middle passage, brutalized by the system of slavery".[10] The memory of "sweet home," then brings to the fore all the brute system of oppression which encouraged the satisfaction of the lowest emotion in the dominant whites. Through all its twists and turns Morrison forces us to feel, what it is like to be thoroughly manipulated by others. She shifts from details of black poverty and slavery to the white world. The 'racial other,' is presented to Sethe's ravaged consciousness as a natural force like snow or a blizzard or storm. The story therefore progresses through flashbacks and recollections triggered at times by other characters, giving us insights into the structure and working of the plutocracy that denied blacks basic human rights. Beloved then bristles with stories of a hapless race, on whom bloody atrocities were committed, stripping them of all their cultural norms and their humanity. It deals with the hair-rising experiences of the blacks that are then caricatured as animals in the national (white) imagination. Although the novel is set after the end of the civil war, yet there are flashbacks to a more distant period, when slavery was still a major concern in the south and the life of the black slaves was bizarre and calamitous.[11]

Morrison dedicates the book to sixty million and more slaves and acknowledges the freedom that each slave yearned for. Morrison's characters stand for all those slaves who didn't even leave their names, who died before they had a chance to become the sort of people about whom you could tell real stories. They stand for slaves (and slaves were not considered human beings) who were not free to choose their own destiny or even love their own kith and kin. Beloved is about slaves unceremoniously buried' without tribute or recognition. It is Toni Morrison's effort to recover the past in narrative, to "insert this memory that was unbearable and unspeakable into literature, to attend to the burial of these slaves, properly, artistically".[12] It is pre-eminently concerned with the outbursts of cruelty on the part of vindictive Father Browns - the planters and the slave masters. The novel talks about the most influential and propertied white men and women who are committed to practices that violate all civilized forms of behavior - practices that are anti-civilization and rather hostile to the well being of the subjugated races. My contention is that omnipotent society is born of an acquisitive urge for money and property. Due to their accumulated capital, they are able to control human beings. 'Essentialized' it means that the white capitalist, the destructive being is still stronger than a simple man, an intelligent being, who wants to bring about constructive changes to end hostility and savagery infesting American race relations for the past more than three hundred years.

The argument is that in this novel, Toni Morrison breaks the continuity of history which seeks to hide within it, the history of the 'smashed and the dead'. What lies beneath this debris is the corpse of humanistic concerns. I will enunciate through my arguments, how the white slave owners deceived or rather emotionally black mailed the poor blacks. They give them a bit of freedom, making them feel that they were actually free men and women, where as in reality this so called freedom is just a bait, a trap to keep them in permanent enslavement, as breeders of more slaves. At the same time, such clever manipulations help them prevent rebellion by blacks effectively. In my discussion of this novel I will also argue through the character of the school teacher how through language and education (and in the absence of a black literary canon) the Whites had the power to originate perspectives to propagate pseudo-realities and myths about the blacks. These myths were circulated to prove that the blacks were sub-human, in fact, animals.

Beloved is set in the nineteenth century, primarily, in the gruesome pre civil war era. In the novel hypocrisy of society is exposed when the story unfolds, Sethe lives free from slavery in an Ohio farmhouse with her daughter Denver, in a house haunted by the ghost of her killed daughter Beloved. This grotesque domestic equilibrium is disrupted by the arrival of Paul D, one of the 'Sweet Home Men', from Sethe's past. This fact then takes us back to 'Sweet Home' where Sethe is brought as a young girl by the white owner Mr. Garner to replace the old and broken hipped Baby Suggs. Mr. Garner the actual owner of 'Sweet Home' treats his slaves well. He allows them the choice in the running of his small plantation. He calls his slaves not 'boys' or 'property', as the custom was, but 'men' in defiance of his neighbors. He allows them to wield guns, to educate themselves .He even allows Halle to marry Sethe and later to buy his mother Baby Suggs out, at a time when teaching a Negro was a crime.

Although under him Sethe was lucky indeed to be married for a period of six whole years to that:

> ...somebody who had fathered every one of her children,
> it was a blessing she was reckless enough to take for
> granted, lean on, as though 'Sweet Home really was one.

As though a handful of myrtle stuck in the handle of a
pressing iron propped against the door in a white
woman's kitchen could make it hers. As though springs in
the mouth changed the breath as well as its
odor. A bigger fool never lived. (24)

Sethe fails to realize that Mr. Garner was only a bit better than other slaveholders
were. His real intentions in procuring her were not really noble. She was young and
could serve his purpose as a breeder in place of the aging Baby Suggs, better. As
Deborah Gray White asserts about slave women between the age of sixteen and
twenty five, "a woman of this age was either pregnant nursing an infant, or had at
least one small child to care for. It is during these years that many slave women got
their best care".[13] Bought as a tender and young girl, Sethe was married at the age
of fourteen. Sethe was pregnant with her fourth child by nineteen. All this reflected
how young girls were used as breeders to further their need for more workers, free of
cost. Although Sweet Home's owner Mr. Garner prided himself of the fact that he
treated his slaves as men and not, men-bred slaves, yet Mrs. Garner betrayed his
hidden agenda, revealing that the most-important purpose of the slave woman was
child bearing. When Sethe informs her that she plans to marry Halle, Mrs. Garner
asks, "Are you expecting already" when Sethe responded in the negative, Mrs.
Garner informs her, "well, you will be. You know that, don't you". (26) Sethe had in
fact been brought to Sweet Home to serve as a sexual mate to any one of the Sweet
Home men of her choosing (which was lucky and exceptional, as slaves could not
choose). She had been brought to replace Baby Suggs, who was too old either to
work in the fields or reproduce. This was one of the agendas of Mr. Garner too.
Therefore, can he be absolved of racial violence wherein he treats a girl of fourteen,
like an animal and values her for monetary gain? Is he really any different from the
school teacher who comes to fill in his shoes after Mr. Garner's death, and who goes
to bring back the strayed animal Sethe when she escapes? Commenting on her
great economic value, the school teacher says, "she has ten years of breeding left,
together with her pickanninies who could be used productively at the
plantation"(149). This comment by the schoolteacher is testimony to the fact that all
Whites treated blacks, whether men and women, as animals. Mr. Garner therefore is

nothing but a moderately violent white hypocrite. Sethe is not a being with soul for them, but a homosapien with a body ready for proliferation.

Mr. Garner's hypocrisy is revealed in its absolute form, when he is about to set Baby Suggs free, after Halle buys her out. Mr. Garner boasts of his kindness to Suggs in front of Mr. Bodkin (another hypocritical abolitionist whose nature can be gazed from the small coin collector kept in his house. The coin collector is a caricature of a black boy with round black eyes and an open mouth, with the words 'at yo service' written on it). Mr. Garner says to Baby Suggs," Did I let Halle buy you out or not? Yes you did, she said, thinking. But you got my boy. And I'm all-broke down. You be renting him out to pay for my way long after I am gone to glory"(46). Mr. Garner had never even bothered to check with Baby Suggs her real name. The name Jenny that he found on the sale ticket, much like the name of an animal on its lapel, he presumed to be her name. And now, like Valerian, he presumes himself to be an innocent God-fearing Christian, even though he made her work for years despite her broken hip and even though he entrapped her son for life in lieu of her freedom. Baby Suggs is agonized even when she is set free, because freedom has come at a cost-the cost of the perpetual slavery of her young, devoted son. She realizes how she became a battered old woman, how she continued to work even with a broken hipbone and Mr. Garner, showed no mercy. He agreed to set her free, realizing that her efficiency had decreased manifold and she was a drain on his capital. Substituting her with Sethe, a young girl of fourteen, and allowing Halle to buy her out, he had only tightened his noose around Halle. He was now in a position to rent him out for a long, long time to pay for Baby Suggs freedom. So inhuman was he that the only difference between him and the school-teacher is that he used sweet words to entrap and subjugate his slaves while the school-teacher used savage, inhuman means to reduce them to a subhuman level. It is, thus, a story, rather a synopsis of the vulnerable position of black women.[14]

In either case, the blacks remained slaves devoid of power and identity. They were not even considered Humans. Despite Valerian's idea of color-blindness, and despite the treatment of his slaves as 'Sweet Home' men, by Mr. Garner, it is amply obvious that both treated their servants and their progeny kindly to avoid the unpleasantness of being without a constant supply of labor. Their socialism and liberality that made them treat the blacks as if they were but an indiscriminate part of the white world, was just a sham. So beneath their assumed mask of color-blindness and humanity existed the lurking evil of power and control. They were not actually disturbed or at pains to dismiss the poor blacks from service when their purpose was served. Immediately after Mr. Garner's death the weak and sickly Mrs. Garner, brings in her handiest male relative, who is known as "school-teacher", together with his two nephews - relatives who are sadistic and repulsive characters. From then on it is all down hill at Sweet Home - an end of the Edenic existence for blacks like Halle, Paul D and all other Pauls and of-course Sethe. Schoolteacher combines viciousness with intellectual pretensions. He is a quintessential figure of the master race, wielding the power of the word as well as the whip. While his students attempt to molest Sethe, this master race proponent tells them to "put her human characteristics on the left and her animal ones on the right and don't forget to line them up"(193). From a near idyllic pastoral life, Sethe is reduced to a chattel- statistic in the record book of the schoolteacher and his nephews. (163)

Mr. Garner at least trusted his men / animals and listened to them, but the school teacher taught the Sweet Home men truth that waved like a scarecrow in rye. Under him:

> they realized that they were 'Sweet Home men only at
> Sweet home'. One step off the ground and they were
> trespassers among the human race. Watchdogs without
> teeth, steel bulls without horns, gilded work horses
> whose neigh and whiny could not be translated into
> a language human spoke (125).

Besides beating the male slaves, the schoolteacher deprives them of their guns and is adamant in teaching them that "definition belonged to the definers not the defined"(190). He is like what Humpty Dumpty spoke:

> When I use a word, Humpty Dumpty said in a rather
> scornful tone, it means just what I choose it to mean,
> neither more nor less. The question is, said Alice, whether
> you can make words mean so many different things.
> The question is said Humpty Dumpty. Who is to be
> master, that's all.[15]

By defining the slave women like Sethe as animals, the schoolteacher implies the power to originate perspectives, to determine the issues, and to establish the field of confrontation. "The namer of names is always the father of things "[16] and to be defined by Whites is to be put in a bag that white America controlled. Schoolteacher too, like Valerian in Tar Baby, denied blacks any subjectivity.

It is through language and because of the absence of a black canon, that the white hegemony was being maintained. According to Sethe, the schoolteacher was teaching things we could not learn. "I didn't care nothing about the measuring string ... schoolteacher would wrap that string all over my head, cross my nose, around my behind number my teeth. I thought he was a fool" (191). His act of recording black behavior, as a measure of his scientific experiment with them, is an echo of what the western literary canon and scientific world was doing. As Kuper says in his book, *Race, Class and Power,* the west was and is always propagating pseudo-realities and myths to prove that blacks were sub-human, in fact, animals.[17] So his definition symbolically defines:

> the violence of western-literary tradition, which is a
> closed set of works, suspending and silencing the
> discourse of the 'other', in its response to human condition,
> a tradition which keeps intact the idea of a
> monolithic homogenous and hegemonic west (51).

By recognizing the resident ethnic culture the white west stands to loose. The schoolteacher uses his reason and wit to form an opinion. He forms a disingenuous and unmanly position and hands it down privately to his nephews "That the Negroes though in their figure carry some resemblance of manhood, yet are indeed no men ...".[18] The Schoolteacher, in his very act of reducing Sethe and the Sweet Home men into animals, typifies the western ideology. According to this ideology the white is the real human race and the blacks that are at the lowest rung of this hierarchy do not belong to the human species at all. Rather the black race is synonymous with animals like the Ape, Gorilla and Chimpanzee. These animals resemble humans, yet are not really humans. 'Race' and superiority of whites is therefore the subject of his education to his nephews. 'Race' structured feelings. It was race that contained the structures of his character and mind, his general process of thought and feeling. "In race, as Taine concluded, was predetermined - a particularity inseparable from all motions of his intellectual and his heart. Herein lays the grand cause - indestructible and finally infallibly supreme". The Schoolteacher is an exponent of this ideology. [19] When Sethe tells Mrs. Garner how she had been brutalized and traumatized by School teacher and his nephews they mistreat her once again "They handled [her] like [she] was a cow, no, a goat, back behind the stable because it was too nasty to stay in with the horses" (200).

This act of the schoolteacher and his nephews is an act of the use of race as a trope to distinguish one human group as human and the other as animal. The sense of difference defined in the popular usage of the term race has been used to describe the difference of language, belief system, gene pool and all sorts of supposedly natural attributes   such as sexual activity, eating habits, athletic ability, cerebration etc. The relation between "racial character" and these sorts of "characteristics" have been inscribed through the trope of race. The trope of race gives "innocent" and "different" cultural tendencies a sanction of God, biology or the natural order. It makes one culture superior or inferior to the other. This race consciousness artificially created, then becomes deadly venom on the tongues of men like the school teacher who engage in a pernicious act of language, to will the sense of natural difference into the formulation which cannot have biological sanction. School -Teacher exacerbates the complex problem of cultural or ethnic difference:

> He uses the metaphor of race in its latent relation to
> power and knowledge aimed to control, by inscribing
> these differences as fixed 'as finite categories
> although fallacious. Arbitrary constructs to language spell
> the difference between the subordinate and super-ordinate,
> between bondman and lord. Its call into use is
> simultaneous with the shaping of an economic order in
> which the cultures of color have been dominated in
> several important ways by western cultures and
> their traditions. [20]

Schoolteacher however does not stop at merely branding the black Slaves at Sweet Home as animals in language. He physically reduces them to that sub-human level. He not only makes his nephews handle Sethe like a cow, nay a goat, but also flogs her when Sethe tries to assert her humanity. He orders his nephews to whip her back into silence. Her body is literally inscribed with the mark of male dominance. When Sethe asserts her humanity, it earns her the scar that forms a 'choke cherry' tree on her back. Unable to bear such excruciating torture at the hands of the white school-teacher, a pregnant Sethe, (after all the Sweet Home men are lost - some sold, some hanged, some imprisoned, some turned crazy), makes good her escape. Being black, to escape the 'tar baby' of Father Brown is not easy. Paul D's escape too, is torturous; Baby Sugg's escape too is painful. As far as Sethe is concerned, she crawls her way to the Ohio River, big with her daughter Denver. She has to crawl and hide herself and drag herself through the forests to be with her children and with milk, sticky and sour on her dress; she attracted every small flying things from gnats to grasshoppers. Her feet are so swollen that:

> She could not see her arch or feel her angles. Her leg shaft
> ended in a loaf of flesh scalloped by five-toe nails... (29)

Further she continues:

> Nothing of Sethe was intact by the time they [she and
> Amy, her savior] reached the Ohio river except that cloth
> that covered her hair. Below her bloody knees, there was
> no feeling at all; her chest was too a cushion of pins (34).

Amy, a poor white girl, who happens to help her during her flight, has this to say about the condition of her back:

> It's a tree, Lu. A chokecherry tree. See, here's the trunk –
> Its red and split wide open, full of sap, and this here's
> the parting for branches. You got a mighty lot of
> branches leaves, too, look like and – if these ain't
> blossoms. Tiny little cherry blossoms just as white. Your
> back get a whole tree on it. In bloom. What God have in
> mind. I wonder. I had me some whippings, but I
> don't remember nothing like this. Whoever planted that
> tree beat Mr. Buddy (who raped Amy's mother and beat
> Amy too). Glad I ain't you. May be I ought to break
> them blossoms open. Get that pus to running, you think. (79-81)

Sethe undergoes much the same torture even after eighteen years as the marks are still evident on her back. The marks, remind her of those days of torture. The psychological damage is uncured even after eighteen years. This is the price the blacks pay to navigate out of the '"fenced in world" of the White Father Brown - loss of self, loss of children, loss of parents, husband even loss of a human face, culture, language etc. Sethe tells Paul D about her incessant pain on account of the degrading humiliation she suffered at the hands of the malicious schoolteacher and his equally cruel nephews. "I am full, God damn it of two boys with mossy teeth, one sucking on my breast, the other holding me down, their book reading teacher watching and writing it up" (70).

"It is a story not to be pass on" (274). The agony of the torture remains forever imprinted on her psyche. The Schoolteacher dehumanizes the members of the subordinate race through his comparisons of blacks slaves with animals and chattel. He denies them, like all other planters, the right to self-regulation or the capacity for self-regulation. This reduction of blacks to animals is referred to as a process of zombification. The zombie according to a Haitian myth, being a person from whom one has stolen spirit and reason, and to whom is left only the force of work. He describes the history of colonization and slavery as a process of the generalized zombification of the subordinate race.[21] That the schoolteacher values Sethe for her child bearing capabilities, and thus for the capital she represents, is indicated both by his decision to capture her and return her to slavery. Sethe comes to realize that it was her apparent value as property that reproduced itself without cost that had allowed her to enjoy the benefit of a pastoral life on Sweet-Home. That she is regarded, like all other black men and women as an animal, is further reinforced when the School-Teacher reprimands his nephews, after Sethe has run away from Sweet-Home, unable to bear the extremely depraved conditions to which she is subjected :

> What would his own horse do if you beat it beyond the
> point of education. Or Chipper or Samson. Suppose you
> beat the hounds, past the point that way. Never again
> could you trust them in the woods or anywhere else. You'd
> be feeding them may be holding out a piece of rabbit in
> your hands and the animal would revert - bite your hand
> clean off (149-150).

So School teacher punished his nephew by not letting him come on the hunt for Sethe (the errant animal) and her pickaninnies, saying "you just can't mishandle creatures and expect success" (150).

His decision to capture and return her to slavery, so that she is utilized in her capacity as breeder to the maximum, becomes apparent from the hunt. Sethe too comes to realize that it was her apparent value as 'property that reproduced itself without cost' that had allowed her to enjoy the benefit of a pastoral life at Sweet Home. Baby Suggs, Sethe's mother-in-law, is also a victim of such violence and she says to Sethe, "[Slavery] ain't a battle, but a rout"(244) She remembers how:

> her hip hurt every single day... But she never spoke of
> it. Only Halle, who had watched her movements closely for
> the last four years, knew that to get in and out of bed she
> had to lift her thigh with both hands, which was why he
> spoke to Mr. Garner about buying her out of there so
> she could sit down for a change (141).

Baby Suggs talks about her sufferings to Sethe:

> You lucky. You got three left. Three pulling at your skirts...
> Be thankful why don't you. I had eight. Every one of them
> gone away from me. Four taken; four chased ...My first born.
> All I can remember of her is how she loved the burned
> bottom of bread. Can you beat that? Eight children and
> that's all I remember (5).

The blacks were slaves, or rather animals, not men. Hence they could have no families. Only human beings had families. And in that world human beings were only whites who needed black "human shaped" animals breeding more of their type, to further their capitalist interests. So Baby Suggs was always prepared for the "dark and coming, better than she was for the life of her children"(139). Just like her children who were all dead and gone, without a trace, without ever realizing who their mother was.

Such was the terrible predicament of the blacks. About the humanity of the Whites, we can say that they were so good and noble human beings, that they 'allowed the blacks to 'buy' their mothers out of slavery. Even a mother came at a price, for the blacks. The price was permanent damnation of the son, to slavery. Sethe too had never really seen her mother. She learns from Nan, a surrogate mother that her African born mother was raped repeatedly by slave-traders and owners. So great was the sense of misery and humiliation that she could not but throw away all her children, a task that normally no mother would do. Once Beloved asks Sethe:

Your mother she never fix up your hair?

My woman? You mean my mother? If she did I
don't remember, I didn't see her but a few times out in
the fields and once when she was working indigo. By the
time I woke up in the morning she was in line. If the
moon was bright they worked by its light. Sunday she
slept like a rock. She must have nursed me two or
three weeks - that's the way the others did. Then she
went back in rice and I sucked from another woman whose
job it was. So to answer you, no. I reckon not. She never fixed my
hair nor nothing. She didn't even sleep in the same cabin
most nights. I remember. Too far from the line-up, I guess.
One thing she did do. She picked me up and carried me
behind the smokehouse. Back there she opened up her
dress front and lifted her breast and pointed under it. Right
on her ribs was a circle and a cross-burnt right in the skin.
She said, "this is your ma'am. 'This' and she pointed, I am the only
one got this mark now. The rest dead. If something happens to me
and you can't tell me by my face, you
can know me by this mark.' Scared me so, I said.'Yes Ma'am. But
how will you know me ? How will you know me ? Mark me' too. I
said, 'Mark the mark on me too'. Sethe Chuckled. 'She slapped my
face. What for? I didn't understand it. Not till I
had a mark of my own.

What happened to her?

Hung. By the time they cut her down nobody could tell whether
she had a circle and a cross or not, least of all me and I did
look (61).

The 'Sweet Home' men and women had worked their heart out for the plantation owner, but what did they get in return? Nothing but the ultimate feeling of being reduced to chattel Frustration, degradation and defeat is their lot. Sethe remembers everything in its lurid and gory detail even after she began to live as a free black woman in a black community, living beyond the Ohio river Slavery was gone but it was not completely erased from her psyche. We have a graphic account of this when:

Sethe opened the front door and sat down on the porch
steps. The day had gone blue without its sun but she could
still make out the black silhouettes of trees in the meadow beyond.
She shook her head from side to side, resigned to
her rebellious brain. Why was there nothing it refused?
No misery, no regret, no hateful picture too rotten to accept? Like a
greedy child it snatched up everything. Just once
could it say, No thank you? I just ate and can't hold
another bite. I am full God damn it of two boys with
mossy teeth, one sucking on my breast, the other holding me
down, their book-reading teacher watching and writing
it up. I am still full of that Goddamn it, I can't go back and
add more. Add my husband to it, watching above me in the loft -
hiding close by - the one place he thought no one
would look for him, looking down on what I couldn't look
at all. And not stopping them - looking and letting it happen.
But my greedy brain says, oh thanks, I'd love more - so I
add more. And sooner than I do, there is no stopping. There is
also my husband squatting by the churn smearing the butter
as well as clabber it all over his face because the milk
they took is on his mind ... And if he was that broken then
he is also and certainly dead now. And if Paul D saw him
and could not save or comfort him because the iron bit was

in his mouth, then there is still more than Paul D could tell

me and my brain would go right ahead and take it and

never say, no thank you (69-70).

Sethe becomes dehumanized much like the Jew in the Nazi concentration camp. When finally the schoolteacher comes to capture her and her children, psychologically annihilated that she is; she musters up her courage to at least save her children. However, instead of attacking the slave catcher and the schoolteacher she kills one of her own daughters and wounds the rest.

The aggression and atrocities is not the share of women folk only, men are equally blessed. The devastating manner, in which Paul D was physically and psychologically emasculated by Schoolteacher, is diametrically distinct from the treatment Mr. Garner gave him. The school teacher created an internal turbulence of opposing movements in his life, with an epicenter that was fueled by tension that propelled him forward -towards the great escape. His attempt is foiled; he is captured by a group of well-armed white men and boys. He realizes then, the ultimate degradation and dehumanization. His feet are shackled, a three- spoke- collar laced around his neck, a bit placed in his mouth before he is tethered to a buck- board and taken to be sold away from Sweet Home. En route from the plantation grounds he encounters 'Mister', the cock on the farm, whose very name suggests more deference than was given to the slaves like Paul D. Paul D perceptively declares: "Mister was allowed to be and stay what he was. But I wasn't ... I was something else and that 'something else' was less than a chicken sitting in the sun on a tub" (72). As his name suggests Paul means something small and insignificant. He does not even have a proper surname. Symbolically it means he was a puny little black, without any history, family to be proud of. It means that he was only a 'small D' and even this 'smallness' he must share with two brothers Paul A, Paul F. Just like he shared his name with them. Such naming implies anonymity and lack of identity.[22] The iron bit in Paul D's mouth is a barbaric symbol of silence and oppression:

There was a wildness that shot up into the eye the

moment the lips were yanked back ... Days after it was

taken out, goose fat was rubbed on the mouth but nothing

to soothe the tongue or take wildness out of the eye (71).

The animalistic nature of slavery reveals itself in the metal bits' confining nature, as Paul D is forced into silence by the rigid, unyielding and constraining nature of the cold metal. Metaphorically, the iron bit refers to the emotional repression induced by Slavery. Thus fettered, Paul D is unable to alleviate the agony of Halle who was passing through a severely traumatic phase after witnessing Sethe's rape. Paul D is rendered mute. Such is the catastrophic consequence of the acts of the icons of slavery like the schoolteacher and his nephews. The apotheosis of his dehumanization, however, comes with yet another experience of enslavement. The eighty six days of shackled existence he would spend on a chain gang in Alfred, Georgia where he has been sent for attempting to kill Brandywine, his new owner. Here his daily life was a totentanz, a death (chain) dance that ended in his symbolic entombment, in a wooden prison at the end of each day, one that drove him crazy, so he would not lose his mind.[23] While in Alfred, life was dead. Paul D "beat her butt all day every day till there was no whimper in her" (109). Listening to the doves in Alfred, Georgia and not having either the right or the permission to enjoy it because in that place the mist, sunlight, copper dirt, the moon-everything belonged to the men who had the guns. Paul D says, that he could snap each one of them like a twig if he wanted to:

> Men who knew their manhood lay in their guns and were
> not even embarrassed by the knowledge that without
> gunshot fox would laugh at them, stop you from hearing
> doves of loving moonlight. So you protected yourself and
> loved small. Picked the tiniest stars out of the sky to own,
> by down with head twisted in order to see the loved one,
> over the rim of the trench before you slept. Stole sky
> glances at her between the trees at chain up,
> brass blades, salamanders, spiders, woodpeckers,
> beetles, a kingdom of ants. Anything bigger wouldn't do.
> A woman, a child, a brother, a big love like that would
> split you wide open in Alfred Georgia. (162)

The opportunity to escape comes during a torrential downpour that converts his wooden tomb into a watery grave, when the earth surrounding the trenches encasing his prison begins to dissolve into muddy waters that seep into the boxes. With desperate comrades, Paul D demonstrates both his resolution and determination at this juncture to recapture his life, evincing, and a willingness to accept responsibility about all that happens to him. In short, what we see in Paul D here is his determination to will his own existence, to achieve being and essence in a world of Absolute Nothingness.[24]

However, Paul D realizes through his life experiences that "definition belongs to the definers not the defined"(190). Paul D represses his hard, unbearable memories in his heart which Toni Morrison calls a "tobacco tin lodged in his chest" (113). This tobacco tin, symbolizes an aspect of the character's psychological make up, tied as it is directly to his slave experience". Like the bit of iron in his mouth, the tobacco tin replaces his heart, the age-old seat of the human emotions. It exists as a cold and rigid metallic prosthesis, rapt with implication directly linking the dispassionate nature of memory repression to coldness and emotive rigidity and heartlessness in its truest sense. Slavery had completely dehumanized him, made him bereft of emotion and feeling. As a result of incessant repression and consequent anguish, that "the lid of his tobacco tin rusted shut" (113), bottling up his emotions and feeling. By the time he got to 124, "nothing in this world could pry it open" (113). Paul D stifles all feelings by shedding his heart in iron, out of the fear that expression of emotions would break him like Hale. He feels that the excruciating pain of the past should be kept located in metal, if he were to survive in life. The metal in the bit, the metal in the tobacco tin and the metal of the chain that fettered him in Alfred Georgia all symbolize the cold, rigid constraining nature of slavery. The metal symbolizes the virtually unbreakable construction of slavery, which completely annihilated the bonds of love and emotions between human beings, by its brute force.[25]

From Son's entrapment to Stamp Raid's freedom, theirs in one long circuitous route of unending misery. Stamp Paid, "born Joshua, he renamed himself when he handed his wife to his Master's son"(184).Even in his humiliation, he did not kill anybody or himself because his wife demanded he stay alive. She told him that he was her only support and after the brutal rape by the master's son, she needed him all the more. After suffering so much humiliation, he is undoubtedly justified when he says that he did not owe anything to anybody. So he extended this debtlessness to other people by helping them pay out and off whatever they owed in misery. He ferried them and rendered them paid for, gave them their own bills of sale, so to speak, "you paid it, now life owes you" (185). All these blacks paid their price for freedom - so they thought to march towards North, the paradise. However it turns out to be nothing but a mirage. Slavery and then the abolition of slavery, in letter and not in spirit, was just another way of oppression. With the coming in of mechanized farming and rapid industrialization, slavery had outlived its purpose. So the blacks began to migrate to the North, to the mills, industries and to war.

The novel captures the momentum of the uncontrolled turbulence of man-woman relationship in the black community. It is a world where "anybody white could take your whole self for anything that came to mind. Not just work, kill or maim you. Dirty you so bad you couldn't like yourself anymore" (251). In the hell of oppression and racism, love and family ties were so perverted that African - American men and women, became thoroughly dehumanized. "Sethe, thought "there was a world out there and that I [she] could live in it" (182) after her escape from slavery to Ohio, where her mother-in-law Baby Suggs lived in a community of free blacks. It is an idea that lasts only twenty-eight days until she decides like Pilate in Tar Baby, that there is no place for herself or her children in such a world. In her community of free blacks she experiences violence when she plans to get an epitaph for the grave of her daughter whom she had killed. She is unable to pay the money to the engraver and, therefore, has to pay with her body.

Ten minutes, he said. You got ten minutes." I'll do it free." Ten minutes for seven letters, with another ten she could have gotten "Dearly too." For twenty minutes, a half hour, say, she could have had the whole thing, every word she heard the preacher say at the funeral engraved on her baby's headstone: 'Dearly Beloved'. But what she got, settled for, and was the one word that mattered. But those ten minutes she spent pressed up against dawn - colored stone studded with starships, her knees wide open as the grave, were longer than life, more alive, more pulsating than the baby blood that soaked her finger like oil. The phrase "Dearly Beloved" itself is striking. It is associated with the opening of the Christmas marriage service - Dearly Beloved, we are gathered together in the sight of God to join in holy matrimony. As a contrast to it she is forced to undergo unholy sex. The over whelming irony and brute violence upon women, is made evident in the displacements of the feeling/emotions inherent in the phrase. Sethe's, personal experiences are so traumatic that it is "not a story to pass on". This idea of unforgettable and intimidating suffering runs through the novel. This opening scene of violence makes Sethe remember an earlier violent incident, when white men milked her like a goat. Of course she had never forgotten it in the first place but this fresh violence rubs raw the earlier laceration of her body and feelings. Such scenes of violence upon Sethe are ultimately crystallized in the final image of Sethe, withered away and emaciated to such an extent that she is reduced to the stature of a child. She is reduced to a helpless nondescript thing, shrinking back as it were, to the womb of her ghostly daughter 'Beloved' who stands besides her. Her story is so horrific that it is not 'a story to pass on" (274). Sethe's memory is "loaded with the past," which she cannot transcend. "Something's you forget, other things you never do" (36). The whites gave her the choke cherry tree on her back when she protests being milked like chattel.   Her back is literally inscribed with this mark of male dominance.   But they were whites who could dirty them at will.   But when a bruised and battered woman who is compelled to kill her own child to protect her from a similar fate, is made to undergo the humiliation of having sex to bury her dead, it plucks the very heart out of her. Such violence is absolutely abhorrent and horrendous. Despair, despondency and a death wish is what such mutilation leads to. This violation of her body is actually a monstrous psychological annihilation. Gender, therefore, becomes the well spring of Sethe's unenviable identity. Being black and a woman is perpetual hell. Their suffering is eternal. Sethe's sexual encounter is, therefore, a direct manifestation of the forces of oppression inherent in black patriarchal society. The unwritten laws of male dominance condemn women to a death-in-life and life-in-death. Sethe is a mere pawn in the dynamics of men, both black as well as white. Earlier the slave masters had the ownership of their 'privates'; later the black men had it as their privilege. Everyone, her husband, her master, her mistress and later a gravedigger - could decide her fate, except Sethe herself.   She had suffered so much that:

> Her eyes did not pick up a flicker of light. They were like
> wells into which he (Paul D) had trouble gazing. Even
> punched out they needed to be covered, lidded marked
> with some sign to warn folks of what that emptiness
> held (9).

Sethe is not fortunate enough to be loved even by the black community. Baby Suggs had thrown a party at 124, Bluestone House, after she was united with her daughter-in-law and grand children. Before Sethe's arrival in Ohio, the black community maintained respected Baby Suggs and listened to her counsel. Her house was a gathering place, the community center, where people gathered to discuss weighty issues that concerned them. Baby Suggs was happy and firmly believed that she belonged to a free community of Negroes, who would love her as she loved them, who would counsel her as she counseled them who would protect her as she had protected them. She gets them to share her happiness.

The occasion of her daughter-in-law's arrival stirs the spirits of the members of the community. The joyous moment begins with Stamp Raid's praise-worthy but difficult collection of a basketful of blackberries. One thing leads to the next and the effervescence of spirits explodes into a feast of pies, rabbit corn pudding, and watermelon punch. A community comprising of about ninety former slaves spends the whole day in uncommon and carefree abandon. But this mood of ecstasy lasts only as long as the day. At dusk, the celebration turns to vexation, to envy, and finally to malicious withdrawal. They, who enjoyed the bold generosity of Baby Suggs', were smitten with malice dark and evil. Their malice had its genesis in the unparalleled luck of Sethe who not only had six years of 'uninterrupted marriage', but who could boast of freedom and children by one man. They come to look upon Sethe as being bloated with self-pride, and see her as holding her head a little too high. She was being contemptuous of them, they thought. Apart from envy it is their conception that Sethe is indifferent to the pain of others, which motivates communal resentment. To get even with her, they deliberately fail to warn either Baby Suggs or Sethe of the approaching danger in the form of the schoolteacher and his band of slave-catchers. This betrayal therefore becomes a 'radiating nimbus' of Sethe's conflict with the community, which ultimately leads to a heart-broken Baby Suggs' death. Those who had enjoyed Baby Suggs generosity were suddenly too resentful to warn her of the coming danger. In her signature style, Morrison portrays the contradictory emotions that drive human behavior. Ninety people enjoy themselves so thoroughly they become not joyful but angry in the end. It is an irony that they savor Baby Suggs liberality, and at the same time they punish what they believe is the arrogance of Sethe with their own arrogance,

The counter-reaction to Baby Suggs feast stems from the same source - the community sees her as unfairly privileged:

> [An] ex slave who had probably never carried are
> hundred pounds to the scale or picked okra with a baby on
> her back who had never been lashed by a ten - year old
> white boy as God knows they had, who had not even
> escaped slavery - had, in fact, been bought out of it by
> a doting son and driven to the Ohio River in a Wagon –
> free papers folded ' between the breasts (driven by the
> very man who had been her master)   who   also
> paid   her resettlement fee - the name of Garner) and
> rented a house with two floors and a well from
> the Bodwins ... (137).

The psychoanalyst Alice Miller says that those who have suffered a lot of misery in life feel very uncomfortable in the presence of those who (apparently) have not. Such people are rarely able to transcend the unpleasantness of their misery. Consequently the freedom of the latter reminds the former of their pain. The only way to survive in such a situation is repression of pain, but the only means to shed the pain is to externalize this pain somehow. But such victims inflict pain on the fortunate and as yet pain free Sethe, who in the view was "trying to do it all alone with her nose in the air". They can not do otherwise Sethe's self- sufficiency and valuing of motherhood draws the community against her. (Weems137). "The community stepped back and held itself at a distance" (177). Ostracizing Sethe and ignoring her presence in its midst, they were taken aback however by what appeared to be Sethe's pride. They felt that Sethe held "her head *a* bit too high?" Her back a little too straight". Eventually, "Just about everybody in town was longing for Sethe to come on difficult times. Her outrageous claims of self -sufficiency seemed to demand it" (171). Ultimately when Sethe kills her daughter the community gets it chance to draw its 'pound of flesh' because they felt that her conduct was outrageous. "You can't just up and kill your children"(256). The community does not seem to realize that Sethe had to kill her daughter because she was once again faced with the prospect of being enslaved by the whites.

Consequently, the community fails to warn her of her approach of the schoolteacher and the slave catcher. Later after the murder of Sethe's daughter and Sethe's consequent arrest, the community deprives her of the communal 'mothering' which it otherwise would have offered. They felt she was too proud and remorseless to deserve it. Envy of Baby Suggs's generosity and of Sethe's youth, deftness and resilience gave rise to meanness. Later they rumor doubts about Sethe's past. Did she really escape from slavery, in her condition? Was Baby Suggs' son really the father of her children? "Ten years later after Baby Suggs funeral, they congregate in the yard, eating the food, they brought and leaving Sethe's untouched." After Baby Suggs death, "Nobody, but nobody visited that house." "Her twenty-eight days of freedom was replaced with "eighteen years of disapproval and solitary life" (173). Sethe is deeply shocked by the pettiness of the community and decides not to compromise. She holds the community in contempt. Ideally, the community should act as a cultural arbiter. But the way it treats Sethe is a slur on its nurturing role Sethe resists its smugness and pettiness. Just as the community in Sula and Tar Baby ill-treats its forward looking and defiant daughters like Sula and Jadine so does the community in Beloved abridge its natural function of coming to the aid of its helpless members. Instead of helping the community hurt the already victimized through spite, jealousy and meanness. As a result, its values and beliefs seem hollow, artificial and constricting to Sethe. Just as the community brands Sethe as evil, so does Sethe brand the community as evil. Later when they do reconcile to each other's ideas the damage already done is extensive.

Even the relationships that claim to provide stability to Sethe are clothed by hollow declarations. Paul D comes to 124, Bluestone House; after eighteen years convinced that he can create a meaningful existence. He declares, "We can make a life, girl, a life". But just like Jude, Paul D is actually concerned with his self-gratification. Paul D's discourse reveals a primordial element in his spiritual and psychological quest: his desire for family, but this desire for family is guided by patriarchal norms. His male vanity gets exposed in after they have sex. Prior to their first love making, he takes Sethe's breasts in hand while caressing her scarred back with his face: Behind her, bending down, his body an arc of kindness, he held her breasts in the palms of his hands. He rubbed his cheek on her back and learned that way her sorrow, the roots to it; its wide trunk and intricate branches... he saw the sculpture her back had became... he can [could] think but not say, "Aw, Lord girl."

And he would tolerate no peace until he had touched every ridge and leaf of it with his mouth (17-18). He convinced her that there was a world out there and that she could live in it. His 'gesture of tenderness', rejuvenates her. "What [Sethe] knew was that the responsibility of her breasts at last, was in some one else's hands" (18). But, perhaps as a man, he cannot fully accept the maternal weight of her breasts. "He held them as though they were the most expensive part of himself"(21). He seems very eager to absorb Sethe's pain, but after the satiation of his sexual appetite, her breasts repulse Paul D. At this moment he symbolically rejects Sethe's, protean identity as woman and mother. Paul D rejects her sagging breasts and feels the flat - roundness of them as nauseating. He feels he could definitely do without such a repulsive body. It is different matter that downstairs he had held them as though they were the most expensive part of himself. "And the wrought iron maze on the back of her body that he had explored in the kitchen like a gold miner pawing in through pay dirt in a moment of heightened passion was in fact a revolting clump of scars" (21) Once his passion cools, despite what she said it did not appear like a tree, although it might have been shaped like one, "but nothing like any tree he knew because trees were inviting; thing you could trust and be near" (21).

> Sethe definitely realizes that Paul D is moving away. She feels:
> May be a man was nothing but a man. They encouraged
> you to put some of your weight in their hands and soon as
> you felt how light and lovely that was, they studied scars
> and tribulations, after which they did what he had done;
> ran her children out and tore up the house (22).

Paul D's dire need for family of which he would be in complete control however compels him to stay on a bit longer. However his desire for family collides head-on with a vanity and egocentrism that emerge from his own insecurity about lost manhood and from the fact that he never had a family. This seems particularly true when he tells Sethe: 'I want you pregnant" (128). Actually Paul D, moves from the position of object in the discourse of slavery to the position of subject in the discourse of masculinity, "Because he was a man and a man could do what he would" (126). When Paul D's subject position in this discourse is threatened (by Beloved's undermining of his will) he reasserts it by seeking to "document his manhood" (128), by trying to make Sethe pregnant.

To enslave blacks psychologically and physically, the whites create pseudo myths about black criminality and animalism. Actually these myths are a projection of their own animalism - 'the jungle they had made' on to the people of color. It is a method of catharsis from guilt. Similarly, Paul D projects the suspicion he harbors about himself on Sethe, replaying schoolteacher's taxonomy of "animal characteristics". He says to Sethe, "You got two feet, Sethe, not four" (185), when he comes to know that Sethe had killed one of the children.   In   this   way   he perpetrates   psychological   violence on Sethe.[26] His words are harsher than his intent, but once they are spoken "a forest sprang up between them" (165). Sethe who had earlier rebuked her community and held it in utmost derision for its petty ways will not tolerate reduction of her self hood and rebuffs ail attempts to minimize her victories as 'woman, as mother.' So she takes back from Paul D "the responsibility of her breasts that she had given him a short time earlier". She says: "[I] should have known better. Did know better what ever is going on outside my door isn't for me. The world is in this room. This here's all there is and all their needs to be" (183).

Sethe had killed her child not out of animal instinct but because she had no other alternative left. Sethe's children, now free, would not become slaves again. "I couldn't let all that [the brief freedom they had known] go back, and I couldn't let her [Beloved] nor any of 'em live for the school teacher" (163). Death, she was convinced would provide a life that was better than any she has known or experienced at Sweet home. Paul D has been enslaved for such a long time and was so used to being deprived of all the things dear to his heart that he is unable to overcome his sense of fear. He considers Sethe's unlimited love 'risky'. Too thick', he said. "My [Sethe's] love was too thick" (203). Paul D, after all the trauma that he had undergone, was unable to appreciate the fact that an ex-slave woman could take the risk of finding an emotional anchor in her children. The uncertainty of a slave's life, which he had experienced, makes him fear such strong expression of emotions. He believed that the far safer way was "to love just a little bit, so when they broke its back or shoved it in a croaker sack, well may be, you'd have little love left over for the next one"(45). Earlier, even Baby Suggs accepted that a slave should not love her children too strongly. When Paul D tells her that her love is 'too thick' Sethe insists that "Love is or it isn't. Thin love isn't love at all" (164). Later she says that because Paul D never gave his 'privates' to a stranger in return for getting a few words engraved on the tomb of her dead daughter, he could never understand the psychic trauma, of a woman, a mother. His advice to Sethe that she could have explored some other alternative, rather than resorting to 'brute animalism' was born out of mentality of a slave which taught him to compromise on all spheres. She had no option. Sethe knew that men like the school teacher, would treat her children like chattel, 'measure their backs', mutilate them, rape them, steal milk from them as a school teacher did with her and later tear them apart with lashes and whips. She preferred fratricide to these 'thousand deaths', which her children would be subjected to, under the white men, justifiably so. She, it was, who passed through the marauding trial. Only she and none else could be in a position to understand her action. She was as willing to die as to kill. "My plan was to take us all to the other side where my ma'a is... who in the world is he willing to die for." (203) Sethe comments about Paul D:

> Paul D is not ready to address even in her story what he
> has learned to repress in his, so he himself falls back on
> the kind of racist distinction between human and
> beast. However, after abandoning Sethe for some time,
> he rethinks the whole issue and realizes later 'how fast he
> had moved from his shame to hers" (165)

He had conveniently forgotten Sethe's tenderness about what he still calls "his neck - jewelry... How she never mentioned or looked at it, so he did not have to feel the shame of being collared like a beast. Only Sethe could have left him his manhood like that" (273). Instead of trying to sympathize with Sethe in her misfortune, his callous statements aggravate the festering wounds of Sethe. He should have tried to make-up for his own "loss of a red, red-heart" (235) by acknowledging Sethe's act and talking to her in a language that did not reduce her to the same level to which the whites had reduced her. But alas, Paul D draws on the readily available discourse of race and gender about romance to deny, repress, project and transfer his loss onto her. Paul D, because he is a male can better afford to accept the norms of white society. Paul D can identify with the role of self-sufficient hero on account of his gender even at the risk (and to deny the risk) of using a racist distinction he also knows can be turned against himself.[27]

As for Sethe, she realizes that once long ago, she was soft and trusting. She trusted Mrs. Garner and her husband, too. But she had come to believe every one of Baby Suggs's last words. She therefore buries all recollection of them and also of luck. However:

> Paul D dug it up, gave her back her body, kissed her
> divided back, stirred her memory and brought her more
> news: of clabber of iron, of roosters smiling but when he
> heard her news, he counted her feet and didn't even
> say goodbye (189).

Irrespective of Seth's conviction that it is her job to 'know what is'; she is not given a carte blanche and let off the hook. She is not only taken to jail but also, and perhaps more tragically, condemned by the black women in the community, indicted by Denver, abandoned by the black man she loves, and haunted by the ghost of the dead child. She is forced into an abject, depressing, loneliness - a kind of "loneliness that can be rocked... It is an inside kind - wrapped tight like skin"(274). Beloved is thus a grisly catalogue of physical and psychological abuses against slaves, especially black women, by men of both races - black as well as white.

At the center of Morrison's novel is an almost unspeakable act of horror and heroism – a woman brutally kills her infant daughter in order to prevent her enslavement by whites. The woman is Sethe, and the novel traces her journey from slavery to freedom during and immediately after the civil war. Sethe makes history by her act. She becomes a historian/architect of change by her act of murdering her own daughter.

The history that stretched out before Sethe, was a history full of trampled and mangled bodies of the blacks. It is a history toward a future that can not be more or less brutal and devastating than the past. The history written by whites crushed and effaced the mashed bodies of black slaves. Toni Morrison, through Sethe, brings us face to face with the excruciating and unspeakable horror visited on black women like Sethe forcing us to remember their horrifying experiences. Sethe, who has been marked, whose body is a site of series of visible markings, mutilations, distortions and violation during the period of slavery, has, as Amy Denver says, a tree on her back. "It's a tree... a chokecherry tree. See here's the trunk its red and split wide open, full of sap and this here's the parting for the branches"(79-80). She has been marked by her position as owned property. Like an animal, a cow she is milked by young white boys and she could do nothing. She did complain about this humiliation (her husband did not come to her rescue). The result was that - "School teacher made one [of the boys] open up my back, and when it closed it made a tree. It grows there still" (17).

Her motherhood inscribes the domination of men over women's bodies. Stamped, firmly imprinted on women's bodies, is the emblem that women's bodies have been oppressed by the world of men - the shape of a pregnant woman's stomach. From conception to abortion, acts which are biologically different and yet symbolically the same, our stomachs are marked mother. All these are marks of physical abuse, brutality, pregnancy, and motherhood by black male and by white male. Sethe is therefore the convergence of these multiple bodily markings. Sethe has to order the past in relation to the needs of the present and future. Her act in the present contributes a lot to shape black women's future. It is developed out of the need to counter hegemonic discourses about women, especially black women that distorted and trivialized women's history, experience and potential acts.

Morrison by narrating the horrific, heart-wrenching story of a mother, a wife, and a woman questions the very existence of relationships in the face of hostile, intimidating outer world. All signs of racial discriminations, psychological molestations and physical dehumanization, strip the reality of all sanity. The humanistic issues remain unquestioned. In fact, humanist concerns are surrounded by a nimbus of inhumanity. Whether it is the whites that maltreat the blacks or blacks that abuse their fellow beings, what is at loss in this game is humanity. The notions of brotherhood, fraternity are loosing their denotation.

REFERENCES

1. Toni Morrison. Epitaph. <u>Beloved.</u> Vintage, 1999. 1.
2. Jan Furman. <u>Toni Morrison's fiction: Understanding Contemporary American Literature.</u> Columbia, Sc: U of South Carolina Press, 1996. 80.
3. Kiz Leppert. "Unceremoniously Buried: Toni Morrison's <u>Beloved</u>." Internet http;//www.ets.edu/eng2952/webwork/kizlepert (uidaha April 3, 2000):n. page., online, Yahoo.com.
4. Walter Benjamin. <u>Illuminations: Essays and Reflections.</u> Ed. Hannah Arendt and Trans. Harry Zohn. New York: Schocken 1968. 96.
5. Richard Wolin. <u>Walter Benjamin: An Aesthetic of Redemption.</u> New York: Columbia UP, 1982. 260.
6. Toni Morrison. <u>Beloved.</u> Vintage, 1999. 6. All subsequent references indicated parenthetically are to this text.
7. Richard Wolin. <u>Walter Benjamin: An Aesthetic of Redemption.</u> New York: Columbia UP, 1982. 257.
8. Walter Benjamin. <u>Illuminations: Essays and Reflections.</u> Ed. Hannah Arendt and Trans Harry Zohn. New York: Schocken 1968. 257.
9. Walter Benjamin. <u>Illuminations: Essays and Reflections.</u> Ed. Hannah Arendt and Trans Harry Zohn. New York: Schocken 1968. 257.
10. Walter Benjamin. "NRe: The Theory of Knowledge, Theory of Progress." Ed. Smith and Gary. <u>Benjamin: Philosophy, Aesthetics History.</u> Chicago, Uni of Chicago P, 1989. 49.
11. Leslie G. Carr. <u>Color-Blind Racism.</u> New York: Sage, 170. 143-156.
12. Margaret Atwood. "Jaunted by their nightmares," rev. of <u>Beloved: Book Review Desk</u>. 13 Sept. 1987: Page1, Column 3.
13. Walter Benjamin. "NRe: The Theory of Knowledge, Theory of Progress." Ed. Smith and Gary. <u>Benjamin: Philosophy, Aesthetics History.</u> Chicago, U of Chicago P, 1989. 49.
14. Jan Furman. <u>Toni Morrison's Fiction: Understanding Contemporary American Literature.</u> Columbia, Sc: U of South Carolina Press, 1996. 121.
15. Caroline M.Woidat. "Talking Back to School Teacher, Morrison's confrontation with Hawthorne in <u>Beloved</u>". <u>Modern Fiction Studies</u>. 528.

16. Leo Kuper. <u>Race, Class and Power: Ideology and Revolutionary change in Plural Societies</u>. London: Gerald Duck work and company, 1974. 84.

17. Leo Kuper. <u>Race, Class and Power: Ideology and Revolutionary change in Plural Societies</u>. London: Gerald Duck work and company, 1974. 85.

18. Leo Kuper. <u>Race, Class and Power: Ideology and Revolutionary change in Plural Societies</u>. London: Gerald Duck work and company, 1974. 85.

19. Caroline M.Woidat. "Talking Back to School Teacher, Morrison's confrontation with Hawthorne in <u>Beloved</u>". <u>Modern Fiction Studies.</u> 528.

20. Charles Johnson. <u>Being and Race, Black Writing since 1970.</u> Bloomington: Indiana Univ. Press 1990. 93.

21. Charles Johnson. <u>Being and Race, Black Writing since 1970</u>. Bloomington: Indiana Univ. Press 1990. 98-99.

22. Wilfred D. Samuels and Cleonara Hudson Weems. <u>Toni Morrison.</u> New York, Twayne 1990. 125.

23. Wilfred D. Samuels and Cleonara Hudson Weems. <u>Toni Morrison.</u> New York, Twayne 1990. 126.

24. Wilfred D. Samuels and Cleonara Hudson Weems. <u>Toni Morrison.</u> New York, Twayne 1990. 126.

25. Leo Kuper. <u>Race, Class and Power: Ideology and Revolutionary change in Plural Societies.</u> London: Gerald Duck work and company, 1974. 13.

26. Jennifer Fitzgerald. "Selfhood & Community: Psychoanalysis and Discourse in Beloved". <u>Modern Fictional Studies</u>. Vol. 39 Nos. 3 and 4 (Fall/Winter 1993). 679-80.

27. Richard C. Moreland. "He wants to put his story next to hers: Putting Twins story next to her in Morrison's Beloved". <u>Modern Fictional Studies.</u> Vol.39, Nos. 3 and 4 (Fall/Winter 1993). 517-568.

SUBVERTING THE EURO-CENTRIC VISION

To circumscribe the plethora of work of a prolific writer as Toni Morrison is a highly unfeasible task. It is highly inappropriate an endeavor to conclude the works of a lining and boundless writer likes Toni Morrison. The claim of conclusiveness to a work of a living writer seems impertinent if not fraudulent. Toni Morrison herself feels that the black artistic sensibility, out of which she writes, gives her novels an open-endedness that resists closure. In fact, she believes that there is no final chord. The readers develop the story along with her and each one tries to find a just meaning in it.

The issues that she addresses in her novels are beyond any final word. All her novels have a certain open-endedness that is open to a number of interpretations. All novels of Toni Morrison leave many questions unsolved. She, unlike, many esteemed writers only presents forth the story and let the reader put denotations into it. The seemingly inconclusive, incomplete or disrupted ending, in which so much remains ambiguous, is highly symbolic. 'And they live happily ever after': such endings where everything seems to be completely resolved are found generally in the Euro-centric literary canon. Toni Morrison subverts such Euro-centric literary traditions by her open-endedness and ambiguity. Whites have completely fragmented black lives. Their 'Look', like that of Yacobowski in <u>The Bluest Eye</u> had conferred invisibility on the Blacks. The whites are hypocritical in their innocence, like Valerian, who is blissfully oblivious throughout his adult life, about the brutalities he has committed. Such people callously loot and plunder African people, to build huge mansions in idyllic Edenic retreats. Such ill treatment at the hands of the whites does not allow Toni Morrison to adhere to the English norms of novel writing and the emphasis it places on closure. In fact, the very process of demarking a society into blacks and whites is a supreme example of humanistic concerns that world has to answer as soon as possible. Her novels by not following the so-called right structure project the need to go beyond all embankments, divisions of race, color, caste or creed.

Perception is a key element in <u>The Bluest Eye</u>: how the individual is perceived or is seen by others, how the individual internalizes that perception, and how the individual perceives others. The interaction of these perceptions helps to create and reinforce the individual's sense of identity or lack of a sense of identity. Some psychologists theorize that the process of identity-building begins when the infant sees itself reflected in the mother's eyes; this gives the child what is sometimes called a sense of presence. This experience enables the infant to see others and to give presence to them. This reciprocal exchange--seeing oneself and being given a presence through the eyes of others and in turn giving them presence-- continues through childhood and adulthood. An existentialist view of the relationship between perception and identity differs slightly. Sartre identifies "the Look" (being seen) as crucial to developing identity. The Look confirms the individual's identity; however, it simultaneously threatens the individual's sense of freedom. The Look reduces the individual to an object in someone else's reality and takes away the individual's sense of self and potential to be. In other words, the Look controls and reduces the individual to the status of the Other. A power struggle ensues as the individual tries to regain control by reducing the "Looker" to an object; that is, the individual tries to reduce the person with the Look to the status of the Other. In Sartre's view, true identity results only when these two conditions are met: The individual gives up the effort to take way someone else's autonomy and to make the person an object or the Other. The individual accepts his/her autonomy and responsibility for his/her own life as well as his/her status as an object in someone else's view/reality. This process may occur between individuals, between groups in a society, and between societies.

In The Bluest Eye, characters in the black community accept their status as the Other, which has been imposed upon them by the white community. In turn, blacks assign the status of Other to individuals like Pecola within the black community. Morrison uses seeing/not seeing and being seen/not being seen throughout the novel. Pecola is invisible in that her beauty is not perceived, and she desires to disappear or not be perceived. The eye is a natural symbol for perception or seeing.

Toni Morrison actually disrupts the continuum of history instead of conforming to its overwhelming linear interpretation. She makes an attempt to re-define American history from a new perspective - the perspective of the oppressed. She does not force the psychological connection of the events on the reader. Rather by amalgamating and integrating the varied experiences of the reader into the interpretation of her story and about history, she tries to provoke a change in perspective. She, through her open-ended novels challenges the enlightenment-influenced progressive historicism, which only validates the claims of the rulers. The rulers here refer to the oppressor of whatever color or race he may be.

The oppressors have always held the notion that the inferior people live on in the very 'Heart of Darkness'. They asserted that civilization meant among other things dynamism, progress decency, legality and rationality. Any being or community that did not fulfill these criteria was termed tyrannical, despotic and barbaric. The colonizers asserted that these barbaric beings stalled the process of growth of civilized societies. So they had either to be eliminated to make the process of civilization complete or they have to be rescued and saved, nay, they have to be educated and enlightened to be made human. In short the rulers have always justified that Imperialism and owning capital is good for the human race. This is the ideology which Macon Dead indoctrinates his son in <u>Song of Solomon</u>. The most interesting thing to note here is that it's the oppressors who decide the authentic, the civilized, and the rational. The rest of the world, the oppressed have to accept it with an undeciphered silence.

Toni Morrison, through Yacobowski, Mr. Garner, and numerous other characters, cuts at the roots of the Euro centric, hegemonic approach which had all the while been exploiting the 'Third world', while maintaining an innocent 'Christ-like' face. She exposes the rulers who asserted that they were helping the so-called backward humans through their robust civilization which was essential for the socio-cultural transformation and technological advancement. However this look, this civilization was actually killing them and mutilating them at will. Toni Morrison shows how the ruler bias violates the very identity of the victimized people. These oppressors with their self-defined values, culture, blue-eyes, blonde skin portray black children and black people, or in other words the inferior lot, generally in a negative light.

The novelist demonstrates in her novels that ruling ideology of control and power is mutilating, retrogressive, and violently repressive. Such ideology is responsible for a Pecola loosing her mental balance or a Sethe killing her own child, a Pauline comparing her daughter to a puppy, or a father raping his own daughter. Toni Morrison tries to debunk the logic of Black bourgeoisie which asserts that the past must be forgotten and blacks should affirm to the logic of modern transnational, color-blind racism and capitalism, which is humanistic. Toni Morrison holds in contempt the belief that such capitalism would lead to immense development of the productive forces on the global scale. Such brainwashed black bourgeoisie foolishly believe that white capitalistic ideology would inevitably wipe out and is in fact wiping out- the gap between the rich and the poor. They wrongly believe that colonization and capitalism by whites will ultimately see to it that all men, women and children, irrespective of class, color or race, be they white, black, brown or yellow will live equally in corporate bliss. The 'Sweet Home Men' may have sweetness associated with their names but their heart were hardened and bitter from the apocryphal claims of living a life of green fields and sunshine. White rulers are creating an illusive but fascinating picture of declining imperialism and ascending socialism. Their statement to forget the past is an attempt by the whites to justify the horrendous violence perpetrated on the subjugated peoples as a 'technical-byproduct' of the process of development. Whites like Mr. Garner, Valerian, try to efface these blatant horrors by focusing on the cultural, material, educational, and social and health benefits that they have provided to this undeserving rabble-lot. The Colonized races must realize that they should abandon their Utopian opposition to the imperialist and must rather collaborate with the rulers, in a common pursuit of more perfect Capitalism.

The question which Toni Morrison wants to ask is 'Can Mr. Garner's claim of being 'progressive in character' and his treatment of the slaves as if they were equal to the whites and Valerian's seemingly color-blind attitude be taken at face value?' Is not the selected and lopsided development of the colonized, actually a means to further use this created bourgeoisie class? Is not the black bourgeoisie being used as agent for the further defense and consolidation of the interest of the rulers'?

Toni Morrison's novels also challenge the Euro-centric literary interpretations of black writing as sociologically interesting perhaps, but very parochial. Just like white history suppresses the voices of the oppressed, so also white criticism has always repressed the structure of black texts. They have always treated black people and their works to be as transparent and immature as to be without ideas. To counter such cultural valorizations which try to stymie black writings, Toni Morrison focuses in almost all her novels how racism and its privileged reading through language imposes its own meanings on black people. The open endedness of her novels is therefore a method to unlock multiple meanings of a discourse. Her novels very strongly expose what Gramci calls 'cultural domination hegemony', where THE people demonstrate that they are superior to the inferior people. She tries to point out that in such a racist world the lesser people have no value unless they confirm to the customs of THE superior people.

Oppression in the form of racism, its most brutal form is explored in the novels of Toni Morrison. The impact of cultural dominance and the violence of language which gives priority to white discourse and denies legitimacy to the black race is also one of the chief features of her novels. The Bluest Eye emphasizes how language is enmeshed within power structure and the dominant social reality. The impact of the hegemonic culture, which completely dehumanizes the black community, is the core of The Bluest Eye. Toni Morrison suggests that individuality especially of the Blacks is certainly not free or autonomous even after the abolition of slavery. An individual, is the subject of a political state susceptible to the forces of control which operate in a given society or social context. After all the control that the whites had been exercising on the blacks can they be termed as free individuals.

Toni Morrison debunks all the claims of the ruling class in her novels. She asserts that the whites have always discriminated against the blacks. The whites have time and again given lovely slogans like the 'melting-pot' slogan, the 'color-blind America' slogan and the 'salad-bowl' slogan. However, such slogans were just clever attempts to hide the grim reality of white racism against the blacks and the other colored races in America. She proves that whites have thoroughly distorted and mutilated the 'individuality' of the black people. Toni Morrison herself experiences racism and it's likely that the experience racism of Pecola might not be really different from the racism she herself might have experienced.

In Beloved most of the slaves at Sweet Home, are called Paul A, B, C, D etc. Paul means 'small', so all slaves are small a, b, c; in short, just not individuals or humans in their own right. In Beloved the schoolteacher chastises his nephew for not putting Sethe's 'human characteristics on the right; her animal ones on the left. Through all these examples Toni Morrison, shows how violent language can be. How language, which ought to be a device for providing guidance or expressing love, in fact, devours people, their traditions and values. Similarly, Mr. Garner never bothered to ask Baby Suggs her name, though she worked for him a number of years. He used to call her by the name that he found on the tag when he bought her. She had a tag on her person just like a dog whose breed or pedigree is mentioned on a tag. Baby Suggs' identity was taken to be the one mentioned on the tag. All such acts show the massive psychological destruction and debilitating impact of language. Toni Morrison believes that oppressive language does more than represent violence; it is violence, does more than represent the limits of knowledge, it limits knowledge.

Toni Morrison deals with the callous use of language in her novels. She says how people, who do not conform to the norms and values of the whites; (values created through the medium of language), are treated as barbaric, despotic or tyrannical. They are treated as a spoke in the wheel of the civilizing process begun by the whites and should be eliminated. Toni Morrison shows in her novels how modern racism does not always require the people' i.e. the whites, to exert overt physical force. It no longer needs guns and the hangman's noose to annihilate the inferior, races. Violence is an impediment to the achievement of a spontaneous autonomous self-identity. The whites dominate the blacks politically and economically. They define and redefine through the media the perceptions and cultural images of inferior groups. All races' and these are methods used to subjugate the so-called 'inferior their ideologies. These are methods that do not allow the suppressed groups to have an autonomous identity.

Psychological violence is evident in Toni Morrison's <u>The Bluest Eye</u>. In this novel all that is 'white' (or Anglo, male, Christian and wealthy) is extolled and infused with connotations of benevolence and superiority. At the same time all that which is not white (or not Anglo, female, non-Christian, poor) is debased and associated with malevolence and inferiority. The white cultural norms lay a great emphasis on 'blue-eyes, blonde hair and pink-skin, as symbols of beauty, nobility, superiority and goodness whereas blackness is associated with evil, moral and spiritual depravity. It is language, through which the power structures and dominant cultural forces operate; it is through language that the discourse of power is constructed. It is language that makes and controls ideologies and social institutions (media, schools and family etc.). All distortion of reality, creation of myths, pseudo-realities, and indoctrination of people takes place through language. This language and its use by the whites, is definitely violent, because after the imposition of white values as 'the values' it creates fractured consciousness. Whites have used language to create horrifying concepts about the color black and have been successful in associating blackness with violence, poverty and dirtiness. The colonizer whites that perceive blacks as uncivilized and animalistic create the hierarchical systems and cultural constructs. All this is done through the medium of language. The imposition of Euro-centric values through language and the politics of control distort the selves of the black people so much that it leads to neurosis. Consequently a 'father rapes his own daughter', 'a mother kills her own daughter'.

The psychological violence and mutilation wrought by the dominant ideologies and its negative impact on the black community. This depraved and extreme embourgeoisement of blacks, leads to extreme situations where the blacks begin to hate their own bodies, their hair and color that makes them different and consequently inferior to the whites. So great is their mutilation by the dominant culture, that it only inspires hatred and destructive mentalities in the blacks. Such mutilation produces in the blacks an unbelievably strong abhorrence for anything non-western. Their inferiority complex causes them to try and hide the dreadful show of passion, the show of nature, the show of the wide range of human emotions. The 'look' dehumanizes them completely and they sever all connection with their culture and with authentic living. To do the white man's work with absolute refinement, to appease the white gods, they go to land grant colleges and schools.

Toni Morrison asserts through her novels, <u>The Bluest Eye</u> and <u>Beloved</u> that Imperialism, racism, colonialism have really not helped the subjugated and the marginal to grow and develop. Rather it has only increased their dependence on the Colonizers for everything and violently mutilated them on every count. The colonized are completely imprisoned and exploited by the whites, who after exploiting them throw them away like a wad of chewing gum. The higher layer of cultural assimilation, which constitutes the backbone of any socialist system or society, is absolutely denied to them. The best of every thing is kept by the elite white world and the blacks are fed on crumbs. They lived being condemned to ghettoes. Toni Morrison derides these society mongers, who tried to equate colonialism with progress. She derides the 'bleeding vengeance' of the colonists who pillaged the colonized people and appropriated to themselves all that the colonized were made to 'sweat for'. She asserts that it was this accumulation of capital that gave the white bourgeois society the material means to crush the revolution every where as exemplified by the school teacher, who employs slave catchers to capture Sethe. He kills all the Sweet-Home slaves who protest against his atrocities, just like Valerian who dismisses his servants with a flutter of his fingers. Temporary privilege might be given to a few people chosen from among the colonized. This privilege serves not only to widen the gap between the whites and the peripherals but also among the peripherals. Consequently the relative position of the marginal, the blacks living in ghettoes is worsening completely and constantly. Moreover such privileges given to the blacks, e.g. the privileges given to the slaves of 'Sweet-Home', are purely temporary and can be withdrawn when they are no longer suit them white masters. Such pseudo-modernization generates social upheavals that subvert all attempts by the peripherals to strengthen themselves i.e. their base. Toni Morrison insists through her works that 'it is not a story to pass on' as Sethe says in <u>Beloved</u>. She insists that blacks who had suffered the brunt of racism cannot, and should not forget their traumatic past. Instead of accepting the white superiority and trying to turn white, Toni Morrison talks of the Black who try to form an imagined community away from white influence. To counter the violence of white racists, her character Baby in <u>Beloved,</u> constructs a home for the physically and psychologically wounded self, where she does not have to respond to any callings. She is acutely aware of the fact that the superior people maintain their domination and control over the inferior people by effectively controlling their worldviews, by selective and systematic indoctrination of their culture on the inferior people. It is this psychological violence that completely mutilates the very paraphernalia of the blacks.

Toni Morrison's novels deal with the double inhuman treatment that is done upon women by the patriarchal norms in explicit detail. Of course, it is undisputed that the real force behind the fractured black lives is the venomous octopus grip of the white hydra headed monsters, yet can we absolve the black men for being so callous and brutal towards their women. We cannot deny that when men like Cholly rape their daughters, they do so because of racism which reduces them to such a state of neurosis that they fail to understand the meaning of familial ties. It destroys the black family set up so much, that they abandon their moral and familial roles, if Cholly's soul slips to his guts, it is because of the 'flash-light' of the white hunters which made a mockery of his sexual initiation, quite early in life. 'Get on with it Niger and do it real good, said the white hunters who voraciously enjoyed the castration of a young boy. He had lost his soul then, and his later act was just a culmination of what had started years ago.

Therefore, Toni Morrison's works deal with how the black women survive in a stifling situation where everybody in the world was in a position to give them orders. Being women in a patriarchal society and being black, in a white hegemonic world, they just struggle for existence. Not even an iota of individual or instinctive expression of pleasure is possible to feel. The sorrow of women like Pauline and Pecola in <u>The Bluest Eye</u> and Sethe in <u>Beloved</u> inhabit Tom Morrison's fictional world. They strike helplessly against the racial and patriarchal forces in the society to overcome oppression. Most of the women are too weak too sensitive and too ill equipped intellectually to openly defy such oppression. These women suffer all insults calmly, just like they suffer the havoc wrought by nature in the form of storms, earthquakes or buzzards. They suffer and embody the image of a black woman as a nurturing, self-sacrificing and infinitely strong burden bearer.

Toni Morrison illustrates how the values of the dominant group i.e. whites vs. the blacks and black male vs. black female become universal values. Imperceptibility gradually but inevitably these values enter their consciousness and regulate their behavior These women, most of them i.e. try to grapple, in vain, with 'the look' of patriarchy and the racists which reduce them to a state of 'thing-hood'. Men who rule over them like a garrison rules over a conquered experiences ultimately, plunge them into the very abyss of 'anxiety disorders', inferiority complex' and frustrations. They are unable to achieve what Alfred Adier calls the 'maximization of ego-consciousness to overcome the sense of lack', their inferiority complex. Their strained ego born out of repression of their feminine 'jouissance is unable to effectively develop a Defense mechanism' to manage their psychic crisis. Most of them plunge in to the very depths of leucosis' where their sense of contact with reality snaps. Some characters like Pauline and Pecola get their psyches corroded by unhealthy introspection. Consequently they withdraw from the world and plunge into a world of fantasy and Hallucination. Pecola begins to fantasize about 'blue eyes and ultimately hallucinates about actually possessing them, while Pauline too fantasizes by trying to dress like white heroines and ultimately takes refuge in religion. It is the severe indictment of the rigidly organized patriarchal society that Toni Morrison brings before us the characters on the verge of neurotic because of the phallocentric order wherein a woman is completely repressed.

The repressed black men make women the object of their frustrations and failed aspirations. They make women's life miserable, drab, mechanical and routine. It is not that Toni Morrison just presents women as helpless and neurotic, she like all post-colonial women, writes to be heard. She writes to try and change the architecture of male centered ideologies and languages. Rather she breaks the mythical, 'mammy' image of the black women in this diametric of power and control women are the worst sufferers. One thing, which a woman can perhaps claim to be her own, is her body, but sadly the patriarchal attitudes have control over her body too.

Morrison's novels refuse to be treated like gum to be eaten and thrown away. The women are denied the basic right of love and respect. They are no more than herds. However, they do rebel but in their own special way. Pecola transgresses into her own dream world. Sethe kills her own child so that the whites may not find another victim. Their rebellion is without doubt, psychologically violent to the men folk. They break and disrupt all myths of women as sacrificing mothers or domineering mammies. By breaking such perceptions and cutting the moral jackets, they transgress into taboo domains of the male-dominated structures of the society. Their rebellion, their running away and striking roots far away from these constricting customs are psychologically defiant acts. They challenge the long held attitudes about relationships between men and women.

The black women suffer from two fronts. As slaves of hegemonic rules, they have to let go of everything human in them and act as subordinates. As wives of psychologically naked beings, they have to show patience to the brutal restlessness of their husbands. The respect and tenderness that registers in the relationship between husband and wife is missing in Toni Morrison's novels. Pauline and Cholly in The Bluest Eye live in the same house but not in each others hearts. Cholly has been stripped of all sense of home and security long ago and Pauline, a crippled flower refuses to merge in the black social fabric. She is happy serving white people who give a sense of being with clean people. This environment is transferred onto the children. The son indulges in wane attempts to run way. But finding peace nowhere he is bound to come back. Pecola, finding no gratification from the family seeks it outside, little realizing that the outside is equally devoid of love. Her desperate attempts to fit in the scheme of things transform her into a schizophrenic. Reconciled into a world where at least one person believes in her, gives her a sense of belongingness. Toni Morrison brings forth the theme of rootlessness in the social existence. Each character is attempting to find a straw to cling on to. Pauline finds it in the white household and Pecola in her aura of friend. Even the colored people who claim themselves superior from the blacks are without any solid grounding. Caught between two cultures they try to live a dual life, thus, fitting into none.

Morrison here addresses the issues of claiming our roots through our memories. The past cannot be altered but it should not be relegated into darkness as well. Running away from our black existence as Pecola and Pauline do will not provide solution to our problem. The society may not welcome them with open arms but a security can be found by having pride in our existence.

The struggle for psychic wholeness is a continuous one in Toni Morrison's <u>Beloved</u>, a novel situated in slavery and its aftermath. It is a process which requires access to painful memories; the characters in the novel reintegrate, achieve "the join" so desperately wished for in Beloved's soliloquy chapter, re-fuse, when they no longer refuse the deepest knowledge of the meanings of their individual and historical pasts. But much of the novel explores the extraordinarily anguishing interlude of time during which virtually all the protagonists, not just Sethe, exist almost as dreamwalkers in a state of dissociation and denial as they remain determined to expend their psychic resources keeping the past at bay. No longer able to endure the endless succession of losses, faced with the death or disappearance of all eight of her children (including Sethe's husband Halle), retaining as her sole and astonishingly poignant memory of her first-born child, Ardelia, the solitary knowledge of how much she loved the burned bottom of bread, Sethe's mother-in-law, the great unchurched preacher, Baby Suggs has a sadness at her center, the desolated center where the self that was no self made its home.. Eventually, she gives up preaching and dies of grief, while Sethe's daughter Denver lives psychically paralyzed inside her own mind. After Sethe acknowledges to Denver the veracity of Nelson Lord's grisly re-telling of the story of Sethe's murder of Denver's sister, Beloved, to keep her from being returned to slavery, Denver takes on a synesthesiac version of hysterical blindness: she becomes deaf, musing in her soliloquy chapter.

While maternal love is certainly one focus of the novel, the male protagonists in this novel also struggle towards a definition of appropriate loving within which they can survive. In the absence of that stipulation, namely, survivability, Halle loves too much, and ends up with his face in the butter; Sethe's companion and lover Paul D, haunted by the consequences of what he sees as Halle's, and later, Sethe's, too thick love, is determined to love small and suffers enormously for the consequences of his decision. Sethe's consciousness, and the consciousness of Denver, Paul D, and the twenty-year-old Beloved (the spectral and apparently embodied adult presence of her murdered two-year-old daughter) are suffused with a truncated, relentless, disrupted chronology common to persons so severely abused that they suffer from Multiple Personality Disorder (MPD) or disassociative states. Despite the fact that she was not captured in Africa but rather born in America and therefore could have no rational explanation for remembering in vivid detail her own ordeal on a slave ship during Middle Passage, Beloved repeatedly returns to memories of Middle Passage, the primal scene for sixty million Africans, the slave ships on which captives suffered and died. Throughout the novel, Denver and Paul D frequently do not know if they are dreaming or awake. Sleep and the comfort of Baby Suggs' nearness protects Denver at night in 124, but during her waking hours, during consciousness, she is almost unsure if she is alive, breathing, in her own body. And in an understated echo of the normal response to profound deprivation, Paul D doesn't know if it is mud or his own tears that are the moisture on his face.

All four of these characters, and, to some extent, every black character in the novel who believes he or she has seen Beloved (as well as Bodwin, the one white character who also sees Beloved), experiences Beloved either as a fractured aspect of Sethe's psyche or as a kind of doppelganger for his or her own feelings of loss, grief, confusion, and rage, and, in the case of Bodwin, feelings of accountability, culpability, and guilt. The story not to be passed on, the story not told in traditional slave narratives, is that of psychosis, dissociation, of climbing out of one's body to forget that anybody white could take your whole self for anything that came to mind. He can dirty you so bad that you forget your own self, however, fragmented it is.

These characters are subjugated to the anti-human value system. Whether at the hands of imperialistic white, or colonizing communities or at the hands of their very own brothers, the major concern is their victimization. Man in the garb of white color, of manhood, or of imperialism is questioning the very existence of his own race. The concerns that arise from such oppression are humanistic in nature. The human that suffers, has the right to live a respectable life no matter what race, color or sex he belongs to. The steely frame of the social machines which forges and fosters the values of subjugation needs to be overhauled. The rebellion is neurosis that has its roots in repression of one's feelings and desires which work against the accepted norms of the society. Some of Toni Morrison's characters make an impassioned plea that they, too should be seen as human beings first and only then as men or women. The vindictive and indifferent society needs be sensitized to the sufferings and psychic conflicts and sense of alienation of all humans. These women show feminist consciousness. They realize that they, are oppressed because they are black and female. The alienation, pain and anguish that each character faces at the hands of society are ample evidence to prosecute society and its ramifications. The loss of family, of motherhood, of childhood, of innocence, of love and of basic respect needs to be addressed. The humanistic concerns in the garb of feminism, racism, sexism, violence are the concerns of the modern day. Paul D's sees loving big as equally dangerous for African American women, and muses to himself that Sethe's large love for her daughter Denver was a danger to her own survival. This idea of love has to be shattered and on its ashes a new world that allows perpetual love should be fabricated. This love will have humanistic lineage and form a society on brotherhood and equality.

BIBLIOGRAPHY

PRIMARY SOURCES:

Morrison, Toni. <u>The Bluest Eye</u>. New York: Washington Square Press, 1972.

_____. <u>Sula.</u> New York: Alfred A. Knopf, 1974.

_____. <u>Song of Solomon</u>. New York: Alfred A. Knopf, 1977.

_____. <u>Tar Baby</u>. London: Picador, 1991.

_____. <u>Beloved.</u> New York: Penguin. 1988.

_____. <u>Playing in the Dark: Whiteness and the Literary Imagination.</u>
Cambridge Howard UP., 1992.

_____. <u>Jazz.</u> London: Picador, 1993.

_____. <u>Paradise</u>. New York. Plume,1999.

_____. "Rediscovering Black History", <u>New York Times</u> sec 6
(11 August). 1974.

_____. Toni Morrison Nobel Lecture
<<u>http://www.novel.se/literature/laureates/</u>1993/morrison-lecture.html>.

SECONDARY SOURCES:
Books:

Adler, Alfred. <u>Understanding Human Nature. trans., Colin Brett.</u> New Delhi: Research
Press - Rupa & Co., 1999.

Andrews, William L. *Three* <u>Classic African American Novels.</u> New York : Mentor
Books, 1990.

Awkward, Michael. *Inspiring* <u>Influences: Tradition, Revision and Afro-American
Women's Novels</u>. New York: Columbia UP, 1991: 57-95 passim.

Bajaj, Nirmal. <u>Search for Identity in Black Poetry.</u> New Delhi: Atlantic Publishers and
Distributors, 1990.

Baker Houston A. Jr., with Elizabeth Alexander and Patricia Redmond. Working of the Spirit: The Poetics of Afro-American Women's Writings. Chicago: U of Chicago P. 1991: 132-161.

Barant, Pauline B. and Eileen Geil Moran. eds Violence Against Women: The Bloody Footprints. Newbury Park London : Sage Publications, 1993.

Barthola, Bonnie J. Black Time: Fiction of Africa, the Caribbean and the United States. New Haven: Yale UP, 1981.

Benjamin, Walter. Illuminations: Essays and Reflections. Ed. Hannah Arendt and Trans. Harry Zohn. New York: Schocken, 1968.

Billingsley, Andrew. Black Families in White America. New Jersey: Printice Hall Inc. Englewood Cliffs, 1968.

Bjork, Patrick Bryce. The Novels Of Toni Morrison: The Search for Self and Place Within the Community. New York: Peter Lang, 1992.

Bloom, Harold, Ed. Toni Morrison. New York: Chelsea House, 1990.

Brooks, Ann. Post Feminisms: Feminism, Cultural, Theory and Cultural Focus. New York. London: Routledge, 1991.

Browser, Benjamin P. Ed. Racism and Anti-Racism in World Perspective. Vol. 13. Thousand Oaks, California: Sage, 1995.

Budick, Emily Miller. Engendering Romance: Women writers and the Howthorne Tradition. 1850-1990. New Haven: Yale UP, 1994.

Butler-Evans, Elliot. Race Gender and Desire Narrative Strategies in the Fiction of Toni Cade Bambara, Toni Morrison, and Alice Walker. Philadelphia: Temple UP. 1989.

Campbell, Jane. Mythic Black Fiction: The Transformation of History. Knoxville: U of Tennessee P, 1986: 136-153.

Camreea, Kren. Toni Morrison's World of Fiction. Troy, NY: Whitston, 1993.

Carr, Leslie G. Color-Blind Racism. New York: Sage, 1997.

Davies, Carol Boyce. Black Women Writing and Identity: Migrations of the Subject. London, New York: Routledge, 1994.

Dixon, Melvin. Ride Out the Wilderness: Geography and Identity in Afro-American Literature. Urbana: U of Illinois P, 1987.

Dubey, Madhu. Black Women Novelists and the Nationalist Aesthetic Bloomington: Indiana UP, 1994.

DuBois, W.E.B. The Souls of Black Folk. New York: Avon Books, 1965.

Ellison, Ralph. The Invisible Man. New York: Penguin Books, 1965.

Erickson, Darlene E. Toni Morrison: The Black Search for Place in America. Dolphin: Publications of the English Department University of Aarhus, 1991: 45-54.

Furman, Jan. Toni Morrison's Fiction: Understanding Contemperoray American Literature. Columbia, SC: Uni of South Carolina Press, 1996.

Gates, Henry Louis Jr., and   K.A. Appiah eds. Toni Morrison: Critical Perspectives past and present. Amistad Literary Series. New York: Amistad, 1993.

Gayle, Addison Jr., Ed. The Way of the New World: The Black Novel in America. New York: Anchor Press/Double Day 1975.

Harris, Trudier. Fiction and Folklore: The Novels of Toni Morrison. Knoxville: UO Tennessee P, 1991.

Holloway, Karla F.C.,and Stephanie A. Demetrakopoulos. New Dimensions of Spirituality, A Biracial and Bicultural Reading of the Novels of Toni Morrison. New York: Greenwood, 1987.

Huber, John Ed. Changing Women in a Changing Society. Chicago: University of Chicago Press. 1993.

Jacbos, Harriet A. Incidents in the Life of a Slave Girl. Ed. Jean Fagin Yellin. Cambridge Mass.: Harvard University Press, 1987:165.

Jaspers, Karl. Man in the Modern Age [1931]. Tr. Eden and Cedar Paul. London: George Routledge & Sons, Ltd., 1933.

Kulkarni, Harihar. Black Feminist Fiction New Delhi: Creative Books, 1999.

Kenyon, Olga. Black Women Novelists: 1970-1993. Lewiston, NY: Edwin Mellen, 1994.

Kuper, Leo. Race, Class and Power: Ideology and revolutionary change in Plural Societies. London: Gerald Duckwork and company, 1990.

Loewenberg, Bert J. and Ruth Bogin, Eds. Black Women in Nineteenth Century American Life. University Park: Pennsylvania State University Press, 1976.

Luckac's, Greg. History and class-consciousness. London: Mulin Press, 1971.

Mbalia, Doreatha Drummond. Toni Morrison's Developing Class Consciousness. Selinsgrove: Susquenhanna UP, 1991.

Mc Kay. Nellie Y. Ed. Critical Essays on Toni Morrison. Boston Hall Univ. of Mass 1988.

Muse, Benjamin. The American Negro Revolution From Non-Violence Black Power. Bloomington: Indiana University Press, 1968.

Oten, Terry. The Crime of Innocence in the Fiction of Toni Morrison. Columbia: U of Missouri P, 1989.

Panigrahi, Mira. Humanism and Culture. New Delhi: Concept, 2001.

Peach, Linden Ed. Toni Morrison: Contemporary Critical Essays. New York: St. Martin's Press, 1998.

Richters. A Women Culture and Violence: A development, health and human rights Issue. Colombus: Ohio State UP, 1991.

Rubenstein, Roberta. Boundaries of the Self: Gender, Culture, Fiction. Urbana: U of Illinois P, 1987: 125-163.

Samuels, Wilfred D and Clenora Hudson Weems. Toni Morrison. New York:Twayne, 1990.

Smith, Valerie. Self-Discovery and Authority in Afro-American Narrative. Cambridge: Harvard UP, 1987 :122-153.

Stember, Charles Herbert. Sexual Racism: The Emotional Barrier to an Integrated Society. New York: Elsevier Negro Digest, 1969.

Trudier, Harris. Fiction and Folklore: The Novels of Toni Morrison. Knoxxville: U of Tennessee Press 1991.

Washington, Mary Helen. Ed. Black Eyed Susan: Classic Stoles By and About Black Women. Garden City, New York: Anchor Press, 1975.

Weever, Jacqueline. Myth making and Metaphor in Black Womens Fiction. New York: St Martin's. 1992.

Werner, Craig H. Paradoxical resolutions: American Fiction since James Joyce. Urbana: U of Illinois P, 1982: 88-96.

Werner, Sollors. Theories of Ethnicity: a Classical Reader. London: Macmillan, 1996.

General articles:

Atwood, Margret. "Jaunted by their nightmares." rev. of Beloved: Book Review Desk 13 Sept. 1987: page1, Column 3.

Baum, Rosalie Murphy. "Alcoholism and Family Abuse in Maggie and The Bluest Eye." Mosaic 19.3 (1966): 91-105.

Bell, Bernard W. "Beloved: A Womanist Neo Slave Narrative Multivocal Remembrance on Things Past." African American Review 26 (1992): 7-15.

Bender, Eileen T. "Repossessing Uncle Tom's cabin: Toni Morrison's Beloved." Bonnie Braendin. Ed. Cultural Power, Cultural Literacy. Tallahassee: Florida State UP, 1991: 129-142.

Bennett, Stephen B and William W. Nicholas. "Violence in Afro-American Fiction: An Hypothesis," Modern Fiction Studies 17, No. 2 (Summer 1971): 200-230.

Bischoff, Joan. "The Novels of Toni Morrison: Studies in Thwarted Sensitivity." Studies in Black Literature 6 (1975):21-27.

Bishop, John. "Morrison's The Bluest Eye." Explicator 51 (1993).

Bowers, Susan. "Beloved and the New Apocalypse." Journal of Ethnic Studies 8 (1990): 59-77.

Clark, Morris. "Flying Black: Toni Morrison's The Bluest Eye, Sula and Song of Solomon." Minority Voices 4 (1980): 51-63.

Davies, Cynthia. "Self, Society and Myth in Toni Morrison's Fiction." Journal of Contemporary Literature 23 (Summer 1982): 329.

Davies, Cynthia A. "Self, Society and Myth in Toni Morrison's Fiction." Journal of Contemporary Literature 23 (Summer 1982): 323-342.

De Weever, Jacqueline. "The Inverted world of Toni Morrison's The Bluest Eye and Sula." CLA Journal 22 (1979): 402-414.

Dittmar, Linda. "Will the Circle be unbroken?: The Politics of Form in The Bluest Eye." Novel 23 (1990): 137-155.

Ghosh, Nibir K. "Prespectives and Challenges." Humanism in Indian English Fiction. Eds. T.S Anand etc. Creative New Literature Series-78, 2005.

Guerrero, Edward. "Tracking the Look in the Novels of Toni Morrison." Black American Literature Forum 24 (1990): 761-713.

Heinze, Denise. "The Dilemma of Double Consciousness." Toni Morrison's Novels. Athens: U of Georgia P, 1993.

Klotman, Phyllis R. "Dick-Jane and the Shirley temple Sensibility in The Bluest Eye." Black American Literature Forum 13 (1979): 123-125.

Kuenz, Jane. "The Bluest Eye: Notes on History Community and Black female Subjectivity." African American Review 27 (1998): 421-431.

Kurtz, Paul Home Page.<http://en.wikipedia.org/wiki/Secular_Humanism.html>.

Leppert, Kiz. "Unceremoniously Buried: Toni Morrison's Beloved." Internet http://www.ets.edu/eng295 2/webwork/kiz leppert/(uidaha April 3, 2000): n.pag.,online. yahoo.com.

Mayer, Elsie F. "Morrison's Beloved." Explicator 51 (1993): 192-194.

Morrison, Toni Nobel Lecture. http://www.nobel.se/literature/laureates/1993/morrison-lecture.html.

Morrison, Toni Home Page.<http://www.luminarium.org/contemporary/tonimorrison.html>.

Morrison,Toni.http://www.archive.salon.com/books/int/1998/02/cov_si_02int.html.

ABOUT THE AUTHOR

Mrs Sumedha Bhandari is working as Assistant Professor of English at Punjab Agricultural University, Ludhiana. She has a teaching experience of more than 10 years and research experience of more than 15 years.

Punjab Agricultural University is a premier agricultural university, working for dissemination of scientific knowledge to farmers of India. The PAU has played a key role in increasing food grain production in the Punjab State several folds share its reputation and ushering in an era of Green Revolution in India.